THE
KILLING OF
FATHER NIALL
MOLLOY

ANATOMY OF AN INJUSTICE

THE KILLING OF FATHER NIALL MOLLOY

MARESA FAGAN & SHARON LAWLESS

MIRROR BOOKS

MIRROR BOOKS

First published in Ireland and Great Britain in 2022 by
Mirror Books, a Reach PLC business,
5 St. Paul's Square, Liverpool, L3 9SJ.

www.mirrorbooks.co.uk
@TheMirrorBooks

Trade paperback ISBN: 9781915306005
eBook ISBN: 9781915306012

Photographic acknowledgements:
The Molloy family, Derek Speirs, Irish Photo Archive, John Carlos, Sean Browne.

With thanks to Gill Hess Ltd.

Edited by Harri Aston.
Design by Danny Lyle.

Printed and bound by CPI Group (UK) Ltd,
Croydon, CR0 4YY.

Dedicated to the victims and families
still searching for justice.

ABOUT THE AUTHORS

Maresa Fagan has worked across a variety of local, national, and international media platforms. Based in the Irish midlands, she spent more than a decade working as a senior reporter with the *Roscommon Herald*, where she first became intrigued with the unsolved killing of Fr Niall Molloy and the many unanswered questions the case continues to pose. Maresa contributed to the recent TV documentary, *The Killing of Fr Niall Molloy*, and has won several accolades during her career. She continues to work in the communications field.

Sharon Lawless is a producer, director and writer living in Dublin. Most of her career has been in the media and she is best known for her long-running TV series *Adoption Stories*, the award-winning *The Killing of Fr Niall Molloy*, the upcoming *Inside the Hospice*, and a feature film and documentary on the trailblazing motorsport icon Rosemary Smith. Sharon remembers the first news bulletin about Fr. Niall's death in the year she left school, and has followed the story ever since. Meeting the Molloy family in 2017 was the spark for her determination to uncover the facts behind the case.

CONTENTS

FOREWORDS

In the summer of 1985, news of Fr Niall Molloy's death in suspicious circumstances passed me by.

In July that year, I was just 13 and ensconced in the Gaeltacht in Galway on what felt like the adventure of a lifetime.

The Molloy case did not come to my attention until much later in my career, while living and working as a journalist in the West of Ireland. I was working as a senior reporter with the *Roscommon Herald* when the case first crossed my desk.

The Garda Serious Crime Review Team had mounted a fresh probe into Fr Molloy's suspicious death in 2010 and new questions began to emerge about what had really happened at Kilcoursey House 25 years previously.

From the outset, I was gripped. The unsolved crime was baffling on so many fronts and begged more questions than answers.

On meeting members of the Molloy family, I was taken by their genuine quest for justice. It seemed inconceivable that Niall's family was still searching for the truth decades later.

A short time after Niall's death in 1985, his brother Billy commented: "I want the truth about Niall's death to come out." Sadly, these words continue to ring true for the Molloy family today.

While this case may read like a crime thriller, it is the lived reality for the Molloy family, who still do not have closure and continue to push for answers, almost four decades on.

It is a case that refuses to go away and with good reason – there are too many troubling aspects to how Niall died and how the case was handled.

When Flawless Films approached me to contribute to a new TV documentary, I was delighted to work with Sharon Lawless and the documentary team on *The Killing of Father Niall Molloy*.

It enabled us to delve deeper into the case and test the evidence, old and new, while also shine a light on the many injustices that have emerged and that cannot be ignored.

It has been a privilege to work with the Molloy family, who have entrusted us with Niall's story and their quest for justice.

Here we detail the many twists and turns and the facts that give weight to their campaign for a Commission of Investigation and, ultimately, the truth.

MARESA FAGAN, 2022

I still remember hearing the first news bulletin about a priest being found dead in suspicious circumstances in Clara, Co. Offaly. As I have relatives in the area, there was instant interest in case there was a link, but none of the names were familiar. I never forgot them though. Every few years there would be a new revelation, twist after twist. It was the embodiment of the GUBU era – Grotesque, Unbelievable, Bizarre and Unprecedented – riddled with scandalous rumours and frustrating injustices. On reading the thousands of documents the Molloy family gave me access to,

I realised the facts were far more interesting than any speculation. This was a story that had to be told, and told properly.

While making the RTE documentary *The Killing of Fr Niall Molloy*, I was determined to show that the priest was someone with a very full life before it was taken from him in July 1985, and he should not only be remembered for the manner of his death. It was important to do the same for Richard and Therese Flynn, but without their family's participation, it was more difficult.

The dream team of forensics experts in the replica bedroom in Kilcoursey brought the facts and still-outstanding questions right up to date. I knew it was a story the audience would love, whether they remembered it or were hearing about it for the first time, and they did. When the documentary was broadcast in September 2021 – four years after my first meeting with Fr Molloy's nephew, Bill Maher – more than 460,000 viewers were shocked, horrified and indignant at the course of events, and the fact the case remains open and unsolved.

Of course, there is always so much that has to be left out for a variety of reasons, including time constraints, hence this book. Knowing the integrity of Maresa Fagan and the trust the Molloys had in her, I was delighted to have the opportunity to work with her on the documentary, and after uncovering so many details that could have impacted on the case, it was an obvious step to take.

This story isn't over yet. There is more to be investigated and exposed and perhaps someday, a witness will have the conscience to come forward and tell the truth, or the government will order a Commission of Investigation to force those who are hiding to speak under oath. Because if the story you're about to read could happen to a good man from a good family, it can happen to anyone.

SHARON LAWLESS, 2022

PART A

THE TIMES WE LIVED IN

Chapter 1
A WEDDING AND A FUNERAL

"O My God I am heartily sorry for having offended thee." He recited the Act of Contrition into the dying priest's ear. Bloodied and bruised, Fr Niall Molloy gasped for breath as he lay on the bedroom floor. Richard Flynn's knuckles were swollen and bruised. His wife, Therese, recoiled in horror and became hysterical. How had 28 years of friendship come to this? How had a summer Sunday ended in bloodshed?

Just hours earlier, Fr Molloy was enjoying, as he often did, the company of Richard and Therese Flynn, at their stately home, less than a mile outside the village of Clara, in the heart of the Irish midlands.

When the conversation was not about horses, it was about returning to France for a holiday later that year. There was nothing to suggest that death would darken the door of Kilcoursey House that night. Within hours, however, Fr Molloy's body lay lifeless and cold on the crimson-stained bedroom floor of his close friends and business partners.

For most people, 7 July 1985 was an unremarkable day. It was a Sunday like any other. After morning Mass, families gathered in kitchens all over the country to prepare dinner, pore over the Sunday newspapers, or catch up on the action at Croke Park.

For Richard and Therese Flynn, that particular Sunday held greater significance. It was meant to be a special family day; the day after their daughter, Maureen, had married. It was set to be a day when the lavish wedding celebrations at Kilcoursey House wound down and family members and in-laws could finally relax.

For Fr Molloy, it was a regular Sunday where he celebrated Mass in his parish of Fuerty in County Roscommon, where he ministered for 10 years. But on that July morning, the 52-year-old cleric unknowingly celebrated his last-ever sacrament before setting off for the post-wedding bash at the Flynns' Tudor-style manor. He came to Kilcoursey House that day to share in the family's joy, oblivious to the violence that would later befall him.

For the Molloy family it was a Sunday that would forever change their lives. It was a day when death darkened their door, not by accident or illness, but in suspicious circumstances. A day when the life of their beloved brother, uncle and friend, Niall, was cruelly cut short.

The events of that fatal Sunday would haunt both families for decades to come. It would taint the wedding anniversary of Maureen and Ralph Parkes and cast a shadow over the Flynns. But, more significantly, for the Molloy family, it would prolong their grief and loss as they searched in vain for answers and for justice.

Today, Niall's family recall how they first learnt of his death. From the very outset, they had questions.

Bill Maher, a nephew of Niall's, who has been the face of a campaign for justice for his uncle, recalled: "My memory, which is just like it was yesterday, was at about ten past eight in the morning I got a phone call from my brother to say Niall was dead. ... The details were sketchy."

"I was shocked so I rang my mother, she was in bits. There were just vague things about there being an accident and because we knew he was so involved in horses, we assumed he must have fallen off a horse, you know, because he was a fit man. He was 52, big build, and fit".

The road to Clara was not a road less travelled for Fr Molloy. Since transferring to the village of Castlecoote in his native county of Roscommon in 1975, he was well used to the 40-mile trip to Kilcoursey House to see the Flynns.

And on that Sunday, 7 July 1985, there was no reason to believe there was anything different about his visit. Fr Molloy was a regular caller to the Flynn homestead; his bond with the couple was deep, so much so that Niall had his own room at Kilcoursey House, where he was considered an integral part of the household.

Their friendship was forged out of a shared passion for horses, hunting and show jumping, which led to a business partnership with Therese, also known as Theresa.

On that fateful summer afternoon, after preaching to his congregation in Castlecoote, Fr Molloy set off for Clara to join in the post-wedding celebrations. The Flynns' eldest daughter, Maureen, had married Ralph Parkes, the son of a well-known Limerick business family, the previous day. The wedding itself was an extravagant affair. A yellow and white striped marquee tent and caterers were laid on to host a banquet for around 250 wedding guests, many hailing from business, equestrian and political circles, from near and far. Prominent political names, such as Fianna Fáil TD and former Minister Brian Lenihan Senior, were among those on the guest list.

Unable to attend the wedding nuptials due to parish duties, Fr Molloy attended the reception later that Saturday evening and then returned the following day for a buffet lunch laid on for around 50 friends and family members. Abandoning his clerical collar and dressed in trousers, shirt, sweater and jacket, Fr Molloy arrived at Kilcoursey House in his Toyota Carina at around 3.30pm that Sunday afternoon.

By all accounts, the atmosphere was relaxed over lunch as the remnants of the wedding wine were put to good use.

During the afternoon and into the evening, Niall chatted with the Flynns and other friends and acquaintances. The gentle and good-humoured cleric even helped to clear off the tables when lunch finished. By 6pm, most of the luncheon guests had left or were among those gathered in the living room to watch a rising tennis star at the time, Boris Becker, take his first Wimbledon title.

As the evening wore on, Niall, together with Richard and Therese, took up an invitation to call to their neighbours, the Goodbodys. They arrived at around 7.30pm, and chatted over drinks about Maureen and Ralph's wedding and looked in on Mr Goodbody's horses. Nothing seemed out of the ordinary; there was no sign of any friction among the friends of old.

Sometime after 9pm, the Flynns and Fr Molloy bid the Goodbodys goodnight and made their way home to Kilcoursey. The Flynns met their children, David, Anita and Zandra, and new son-in-law Ralph, along the road. Both cars stopped briefly as the twenty-somethings headed to White's pub to round off the weekend celebrations.

Back at Kilcoursey, newlywed Maureen and her sister-in-law, Ann, were keeping an elderly relative, Auntie May, company but soon left to join the rest of the wedding party. James Lowry, the young groom employed at Kilcoursey, was also at the house briefly, having returned to change his clothes before going out for the night.

Meanwhile, Niall, Richard and Therese continued to chat over another drink or two before calling it a night. They discussed plans to return to Normandy for a holiday, possibly that September.

At around midnight a nightcap was mooted. The conversation carried over into Richard and Therese's bedroom, which adjoined Niall's room. What they talked about remains unclear.

A short time later, Niall and Therese lay stretched out and unconscious on the floor of the master bedroom.

Richard had struck both of them. Therese was breathing when he checked but Niall was having difficulty. He threw water on their faces hoping to revive them.

The 47-year-old businessman then recited the Act of Contrition into Niall's ear before going downstairs to call the family doctor and local priest. Back in the master bedroom, Therese came round but was dazed. She saw Fr Molloy lying on the floor and thought he had passed out. When he showed no vital signs, Therese tried to give her friend and business partner the kiss of life. Her attempts, however, were in vain. When Richard returned from downstairs, he found his wife in a state of hysteria as she struggled to understand what had happened.

By this point, Richard had summoned the parish priest, Fr James Deignan, who lived in the parochial house, Drayton Villa, a few hundred yards away.

It was around 1am when Fr Deignan, who had officiated at the weekend wedding, arrived at Kilcoursey. Aside from the obvious injuries sustained by Fr Molloy, there were bloodstains throughout the bedroom and a bloody streak on the carpet that was several feet long – all screaming out for an explanation. Fr Deignan didn't ask for one, however, and none was offered.

He administered the Last Rites to Niall before leaving for the parochial house in search of his glasses. By the time he returned, some of the wedding party revellers had arrived back from the pub.

Newlyweds Maureen and Ralph, along with Anita and Zandra Flynn, returned to the sobering news of Fr Molloy's death. David Flynn and his wife, Ann, were at their home in Tober, a few miles away, but made their way to Kilcoursey a short time later when they heard the news. It was a terrible accident, they were told.

Maureen went up to her parents' bedroom to find the awful scene – Fr Molloy lying on his back with a pool of blood at his head and her mother frantically trying to bring him back to life.

As a trained nurse, Maureen checked Niall's pulse but could not find one. She closed his eyes and covered his face with a towel before placing his arm over his chest. She then turned her attention to her mother, Therese, who was hysterical and had to be restrained.

Downstairs, further efforts were made to reach the family GP but without success. Around half an hour later, Fr Deignan drove Zandra to Kilbeggan to inform Dr Daniel O'Sullivan of the death at Kilcoursey.

Sometime after 2am, Dr O'Sullivan arrived at the Flynn home, where he recognised the man lying on the bedroom floor as Fr Molloy, and confirmed that he was dead. Finding Therese in a state of hysteria, he gave her sedatives before deciding to take her to Tullamore Hospital, accompanied by her daughters, Maureen and Anita. Before leaving, he asked Fr Deignan to contact the Gardaí.

Another significant period of time would pass, however, before the Gardaí were informed of the badly beaten clergyman, who now lay dead in the Flynns' master bedroom.

Fr Deignan chatted with family members and spoke privately with Richard to discover it was a fellow priest who lay dead upstairs.

This was the account given by Richard and Therese Flynn and other witnesses present on the night Fr Molloy died – an account of events that was never tested in court or at Niall's inquest and that will be probed in the following chapters.

It was 3.15am before Fr Deignan knocked on the door of Clara Garda Station to rouse Sergeant Kevin Forde and alert him of the death at Kilcoursey House. The man had died in an accident, Fr Deignan said, asking the local sergeant if there was any way to keep the "terrible scandal" quiet.

A dead priest in the bedroom of a wealthy couple was not something that Sgt Forde was accustomed to but he quickly ruled out hushing up any scandal. He told Fr Deignan that the death would have to be investigated and he immediately alerted the acting District Officer for the Tullamore area.

At around 3.30am, Sgt Forde arrived at Kilcoursey House, several hours after Fr Molloy received a number of blows to the head. On reaching the bedroom, he saw the dead priest lying on his back, fully clothed, and with a towel concealing his face. On lifting it, he noticed the priest had a burst lip and cut to his jaw; there was blood on Niall's face.

The local sergeant immediately preserved the scene and noted the pool of blood at Fr Molloy's head and the long streak of blood that suggested the body was moved or dragged across the room. The bed was in disarray but there was no apparent sign of a struggle anywhere. Blood smears were evident in the bedroom and ensuite bathroom and also on the stair banister. In the adjoining bedroom, a cigar butt and glass of milk sat on a bedside locker. Downstairs, a dining table and glass-topped coffee table lay damaged.

In the sitting room, Sgt Forde spoke to Richard Flynn, who appeared calm and unconcerned. Referring to Niall's death as a "messy old business", the businessman apologised for bringing the local sergeant out at such an hour.

By this stage, Garda Inspector Thomas Monaghan, acting District Officer for Tullamore, had arrived at the house. During a brief interview, Richard told the two Garda officers that he was "the culprit" and admitted to striking his wife and Fr Molloy.

Richard dismissed any suggestion that his wife and Niall were found in a compromising position but claimed they had attacked him after a "stupid argument" erupted over drink. Responding to the alleged attack, Richard said he hit back, rendering both of them unconscious. His wife revived but Fr Molloy did not.

During this initial interview, Richard also told Gardaí that Fr Molloy had difficulty breathing and suggested the 52-year-old cleric had a heart condition.

Gardai did not interview anyone else in Kilcoursey House that night. Therese had already left the house for Tullamore Hospital by the time Gardaí arrived at the crime scene.

As a new day dawned, Garda set up an incident room in Tullamore Garda Station as the wheels were set in motion for a full investigation into the unexplained death.

It was after 5am when Sgt Forde and Inspector Monaghan left Kilcoursey House, while more Gardaí were dispatched from Tullamore, Clara and Dublin to preserve the scene for technical and forensic examination.

The following day, Fr Molloy's remains were taken to the morgue at Tullamore General Hospital for a post-mortem examination by State Pathologist Dr John Harbison.

As Gardaí continued their enquiries that Monday, Inspector Monaghan returned to Kilcoursey hoping to take a fresh statement from Richard. On legal advice, Richard declined and Gardaí had little option but to rely on the information he had already relayed to them the previous night.

Gardaí were left none the wiser when on the morning of 9 July, Therese Flynn told them from her hospital bed in Tullamore that she could not recall what had happened. She had gone to bed a little earlier than her husband and Fr Molloy and had taken a sleeping pill, she said. The next thing she remembered was seeing Fr Molloy lying on the bedroom floor and then trying, unsuccessfully, to resuscitate him. That was all she could recall.

At the time, Gardaí had limited powers of arrest and detention. Under the 1939 Offences against the State Act, they could only detain and question someone suspected of subversive activity or murder involving a firearm. These powers did not extend to other serious crimes, such as manslaughter or serious assault, leaving Gardaí with the limited option of inviting suspects to speak to them on a voluntary basis. Faced with Fr Molloy's unexplained death, Gardaí were met with a wall of silence in the days and weeks that followed. They were unable to interview members of the Flynn family about events on the night that he died and instead received statements prepared by the family solicitor on 14 July. This was in keeping with the law but was less than helpful to the Garda investigation. The prepared statements provided a version of events that would ultimately be presented before the courts and would go largely unchallenged.

As news of Fr Molloy's demise reached County Roscommon, it was all too much for his family and parishioners to take in. Was it a car crash? Was he thrown from a horse? These were the first thoughts that came to Fr Molloy's elder brother, Billy. He was at home in Castlerea when his local parish priest knocked on the door to break the tragic news. He was initially told that Fr Molloy died after an accident at Kilcoursey House. On hearing what had happened, Billy broke down in tears in front of his family. The brothers were close; Niall was the youngest of the nine Molloy children and there was 10 years between them. Fr Molloy always went to Castlerea for Christmas dinner with Billy's family. Billy last saw him at a horseshow outside Roscommon town a week earlier. Now he was told his brother was dead.

Billy, an entrepreneur, never met the Flynns but knew of Niall's friendship with them. He could not understand how his brother, an active and healthy man in the prime of his life, could be dead. Suggestions that it was an accident or that Niall had a heart condition were even more confusing. Billy needed answers and, to that end, he set off for County Offaly that day, once the initial shock subsided.

At Kilcoursey House, Richard told Billy he was "so sorry" about what had happened to his brother. He told Billy that a lot of drink was taken on the night and that a political argument had taken place downstairs. He suggested that Fr Molloy had fallen and hit his head.

Seeking more answers, Billy asked what happened next. And with that, there was a knock on the door and one of the Flynn daughters intervened to offer coffee. Billy declined and left the house immediately, his suspicions further roused. Within days of his visit to Kilcoursey, Billy made a statement to Gardaí about the alleged political row that Richard had claimed occurred on the day Niall died.

Still reeling from the shock of Fr Molloy's untimely death and the unusual circumstances in which he was found, his family took on the difficult task of arranging his funeral.

On Wednesday, 10 July, Fr Molloy's family, friends and parishioners crammed into the Church of the Assumption in the rural village of Castlecoote, preparing to say goodbye to the gentle and much-loved curate.

As his remains were removed from Smyths Funeral Home in Roscommon town, members of Roscommon Equestrian Club and Roscommon Hunt lined the route. Arriving into the village he had served for a decade, the funeral cortege was met by no less than two guards of honour.

It was a particularly poignant funeral for Tom Smyth, the undertaker, who was a close personal friend of Fr Molloy's, having worked closely with him in the parish over the years.

Just days before, they were both attending a funeral in Athleague on the morning of the Kilcoursey wedding when Fr Molloy sat into the funeral car and confided that he did not want to go to the wedding celebrations. "I dread going up there but I know I have to," he told Tom.

On the day of Fr Molloy's funeral, hundreds of people turned out to pay respect to the man known to many as the 'smiling priest'. The clergy was also well represented, with as many as 100 priests from his Diocese of Elphin in attendance.

Distraught and inconsolable, the Molloy family took some small comfort from the large turnout at Niall's funeral and the high esteem in which he was held.

One letter of sympathy from the Pope's General Secretary, Fr John Magee, described Fr Molloy as a "truly zealous priest and a credit to the Irish College in Rome".

During the funeral Mass, the chief celebrant Bishop of Elphin, Dominic Conway, said Fr Molloy's tragic death had filled everyone with a deep sense of loss. "Everyone loved Fr Niall and his death brings a big sadness," the Bishop told the congregation.

In the funeral homily, Fr Molloy's friend and former classmate, Fr James Casey, paid tribute to the quiet cleric: "As a boy he was the gentlest in his class. He never raised his voice even when provoked. Niall never lost that gentleness, that winning smile of his."

"His kindness and sensitivity manifested itself in his treatment of all God's creatures. A great lover of horses as a young man he proved himself to be an expert showjumper," Fr Casey added.

Referring to Fr Molloy's time as Army Chaplain, he added that his friend and fellow clergyman was respected by all who knew him: "Again, Fr Niall's quiet kindness and gentleness won for him the respect of all. He was nature's gentleman and even the rawest recruit came to know him and respect him as such."

Fr Molloy, he said, had put his "heart and soul" into developing a community centre for local youths and his work within the parish.

The funeral was also attended by members of the Flynn family, who attracted much attention from reporters and photographers as they left the small churchyard. The hungry media pack, however, failed to elicit any comment from Richard.

More than three decades on, the shock and disbelief triggered by Niall's untimely and violent death remain etched in the minds of the Molloy family.

"I remember the massive crowds and just thinking they're all here because of a gentle priest who touched their lives with gentleness," Fr Billy Molloy, who followed in his uncle's footsteps into the priesthood, recalls.

"In some ways I felt lost because I couldn't get my head around the gravity of what had happened, the shock of what had happened," he added.

As the family grappled with grief, their loss was made all the more difficult by the circumstances in which he was found. The discovery of a badly beaten priest in the bedroom of a well-heeled couple was enough to send the rumour mill into overdrive. Newspapers at home and abroad carried details of the priest's suspicious death. 'Society wedding that ended in tragedy', 'Priest's mystery death at wedding', 'Gardaí keep open mind on death of priest' – the media interest and coverage was insatiable.

His death became the talk of the nation. There was much speculation and titillation, such as rumours of an affair – all baseless. The gossip was hurtful and cruel for both families involved and fuelled calls for the establishment of a press council to deal with complaints about media coverage, at the monthly meeting of Roscommon County Council.

Local Fianna Fáil TD and council member, Terry Leyden, who was also a parishioner of Fr Molloy's, led the charge and castigated elements of the media for their "insensitive" coverage of the tragedy.

"It is sad that the media have dealt with his death by innuendo. There is so much suffering involved it is unforgivable. A press council should be established in this country as an avenue whereby the people could express their abhorrence at the abuse of such a powerful priest in this manner," Deputy Leyden said.

"Outrage over priest death riddle reports," a front page story in the *Roscommon Champion* on 19 July stated, as it detailed the local reaction to news coverage of Niall's death.

Fr Edward Jones, who replaced Fr Molloy as Fuerty parish priest, described his friend as a "good, humble and holy man", and also lashed out at media reports. "At a time of great personal stress and grief, the powerful media should show a little humanity and sympathy and understanding to those who are already suffering more than enough," he said.

He took exception, in particular, to "the implications of personal involvements" in some press reports.

Within weeks of Niall's death, Billy Molloy told a local newspaper of the family's upset by some of the "grievously harmful" headlines but that they remained keen for the "whole truth" to come out. "I want the full facts to be made known so that Niall's name, which has been smeared by insinuations in press reports of his death, can be cleared," he told the *Roscommon Champion*.

After the funeral, the still stunned Molloy family began to question how Niall may have died and what might have happened at Kilcoursey House. Niall was not always forthcoming about his business affairs or friendship with the Flynns but as family members began to talk to each other they learnt that this friendship had been on the wane for months.

Earlier that year, Niall told a cousin, Martin Molloy, that he wished to sever ties with the Flynns and switch from trading in horses to focus on cattle.

A week after Niall's death, another shocking revelation emerged. Family members learned that he was owed money by the Flynns after plans to buy land from Richard fell through.

The revelations came to light when Fr Molloy's relatives spoke to a solicitor, who had acted for Niall and Therese over several years. It appeared that after the deal collapsed, Fr Molloy was anxious to see the return of the sizeable deposit he had paid over.

This pertinent new information was relayed to Gardaí, who took the matter seriously and considered it as a motive for Fr Molloy's death.

Days later, on 19 July, Gardaí called to Kilcoursey House to interview Richard about the land deal and the alleged monies owed to Fr Molloy. They put it to him that Niall had expressed serious concern about getting a large sum of money back but the business-man declined to make a statement without his solicitor.

Four days later, Gardaí returned to Kilcoursey in search of answers but Richard again refused to be interviewed or to make a statement. Therese, however, attempted to provide some clarity and claimed to have repaid IR£11,000 to Fr Molloy months before he died.

Gardaí spoke to Niall's solicitor about the land deal and while they had difficulty accepting that a "stupid argument" over drink could lead to such a violent attack, the money trail was not pursued further at that stage, even though it was cited as a possible motive in the Book of Evidence. No statement appeared from the solicitor in relation to the deal and outstanding money.

In the meantime, members of the Molloy family continued to make their own enquiries and seek answers. When Billy Molloy received Niall's personal effects, some fresh concerns emerged.

Among the personal items returned to the family was a gold Favre-Leuba watch. The face of the expensive wrist watch was cracked but the hands were stuck at 10.40, possibly yielding another clue as to what happened on that fateful night. Could it have been broken during the row, which Richard claimed had taken place after midnight?

As the weeks went by, the Molloy family grew anxious over the pace of the Garda investigation and the length of time it was taking to press charges.

Niall's brother, Billy, visited Tullamore Garda Station on numerous occasions seeking updates in the case but to no avail. "Almost a month has elapsed since I was given the terrible news. What upsets me most is that I have lost a brother and I have been given no information about how he died," Billy told a local newspaper.

"I know the Gardaí have been working very hard, have been very understanding towards my family, and are trying to clear it up as quickly as they can. When they do, I hope they will let myself and the public know the truth," he said.

"Many tears were shed and will be shed whenever talk of Fr Niall comes to our lips. The sooner the facts are known, the sooner we will be put at ease," he added.

Within a matter of days, there were reports in local and national media of Gardaí experiencing difficulties in preparing a file for the Director of Public Prosecutions (DPP).

The Irish Times reported a delay in obtaining the post-mortem report due to holiday leave and that Gardaí had failed to establish a clear motive for the incident that led to Fr Molloy's death.

While concerns over the Flynns' financial situation were now in the public domain, it was reported that Gardaí found it hard to access information about the joint bank account or accounts held by Fr Molloy and Therese Flynn.

Meanwhile, RTE's flagship current affairs programme *Today Tonight* took an interest in the case and in late August aired a short segment remembering Niall as a "man of outstanding character and integrity".

In advance of the broadcast, the community of Castlecoote gathered in Golden's pub in the village to express solidarity with the Molloy family and to put their own thoughts about their beloved curate on the record.

In a media statement issued after the closed meeting, parishioners said: "He will always be remembered for his gentleness, kindness and wonderful gift of consoling people in grief. We turned to him in joy and sorrow, assured that in him we would find a sincere and devoted friend."

"Fuerty is now a lonely parish without the holy and humble presence of Fr Niall but we will be forever grateful to the Molloy family for the privilege of having his remains resting in our Church grounds amidst the shrubs and plants which he proudly planted and nurtured himself," the statement added.

Around seven weeks after the priest's death, Richard Flynn was charged with assault causing harm and the unlawful killing of Fr Molloy between 9pm on 7 July and 2.30am the following morning. He personally collected the summonses from the Garda station on his return from a holiday in France.

The news brought mixed emotions for Billy and the Molloy family. On learning of the charges, Billy commented: "We were glad to hear that the file is being released and that we will be able to clear my brother's name. It takes a lot of pressure off us but a charge of manslaughter will never be accepted by us."

In the months that followed, Kilbeggan District Court in Westmeath became the focus of local, national and international media attention. For news editors, the case was dynamite. As one writer for the UK-based *Observer* newspaper suggested, the trial had the potential to rival the popular TV show *Dynasty* with its "rich mix of religion, high finance, horse breeding and even politics". Mention of the TV drama, *The Thorn Birds*, where a priest and a woman had an illicit relationship, proved to be hurtful and upsetting for Fr Molloy's family and friends as it was not the act of the man they knew and loved.

It was late September when Richard made his first court appearance in Kilbeggan Courthouse. The tiny room was packed; relatives of Fr Molloy were joined by parishioners from Castlecoote, a massive media presence, as well as gawkers and gossipers, all keen to find out what happened. The Bishop of Elphin Dominic Conway and Fr Cyril Harron from the diocese were also among the clergy in attendance during the preliminary hearings.

Despite rain that day, large numbers of locals watched from street corners and cameras were at the ready to report the outcome as soon as it happened.

The expectation was short-lived though, as the hearing lasted less than a minute. State Solicitor for Offaly, Jim Houlihan, sought extra time to prepare the Book of Evidence. Judge William Tormey remanded Mr Flynn to appear again a month later.

The following day, Fr Molloy's brother, Billy, wrote to local Fine Gael TD Liam Naughten, expressing concern again over how Niall's death was being handled.

"Fr Niall was murdered 12 weeks ago, still no Book of Evidence ready while his partners can sell off his stock (even under the police) at the RDS for £64,000. His murderer, Mr Flynn, who told us he killed him is let off on holidays," Billy wrote.

"Liam, please pass my letter on to your (illegible text) friends and raise the question in the House in force. Publicity and pressure on the courts is all that's left," he added, before signing off in an air of desperation: "Please help us."

When the case returned to the courthouse in Kilbeggan in October, interest had not abated. The case, however, was put back again, when Mr Flynn's solicitor, Liam Lysaght, sought a four-week adjournment citing "complex matters of fact in law" and the need for more time to read the Book of Evidence.

It was on Richard's third court appearance on a cold November day that Judge William Tormey returned him for trial to Tullamore Circuit Court the following spring.

On reading the Book of Evidence, Judge Tormey said there was a "sufficient case" for the accused to stand trial on charges of manslaughter and assault causing harm.

Richard was remanded on bail on a bond of IR£100 and was free to go.

Despite the media glare, the accused businessman appeared composed and calm. Throughout these brief court appearances, he failed to show any emotion and at times was observed reading a newspaper while waiting for the case to be mentioned.

When the February court date finally came round, the case was transferred to Dublin on the request of Flynn's solicitor, although the reasons for the transfer remain unclear.

Judge Thomas Frank Roe, who was well known in horse racing circles and had close ties to Fine Gael, would preside over the case now listed for June 1986 and expected to last several days.

In the intervening months, more questions arose about what happened at Kilcoursey House that night. Members of the Molloy family were left wondering why nobody called an ambulance or dialled 999. They wondered why it took several hours to alert Gardaí to the body of Niall. They wondered why the priest's body was moved. They wondered about the monies owed to Niall after the land deal fell through. They wondered about the time on his watch and whether he had died much earlier. These were all obvious and relevant questions that they believed would be answered when the case came to trial. A year later, however, they would be bitterly disappointed.

Chapter 2

AN EXTRAORDINARY
INTERVENTION

Almost a year after Fr Niall Molloy's death, the June trial date came around. The transfer to Dublin did nothing to quell interest in the high-profile case.

In the case of the Director of Public Prosecutions versus Richard Flynn, the businessman was due to stand trial for manslaughter and assault and there was an air of expectation and tension.

The Molloy family hoped the trial would be a day of reckoning after months of wild speculation. Friends and parishioners of the dead priest, who travelled in convoy from Castlecoote, hoped the trial would shed light on events in Kilcoursey House that night. Church representatives were also in attendance.

As the trial opened, the press gallery was packed with reporters from near and far, eager to satisfy the insatiable public appetite for details of what really happened.

As in previous court appearances, Richard was flanked by his family and appeared unmoved by proceedings.

The court case was expected to take a number of days. In a matter of hours, however, the trial was sensationally cut short.

###

On Thursday, 12 June 1986, there was standing room only in Courtroom No 14 at Dublin Circuit Criminal Court, where the Flynn trial was due to open.

Judge Thomas Frank Roe, who earlier that year was appointed President of the Circuit Court, was presiding over the trial.

Mr Flynn's defence team was led by Patrick McEntee, a hugely successful and well-regarded senior counsel, who had acted in several high-profile cases by the mid-1980s. He was supported by John Connolly BL.

The prosecution was represented by Raymond Groarke BL, who would years later serve as a Circuit Court Judge and President of the Circuit Court.

When the charges of manslaughter and assault were put to Richard Flynn, the 48-year-old denied them both.

The accused businessman was accompanied in court by his daughter, Maureen, son David, and daughters Zandra and Anita. His wife Therese was not present for the trial.

At the time, spouses could not by law be compelled to give evidence against their partners but within months of the trial the Law Reform Commission recommended abolishing this outdated law.

In his opening address, the prosecuting counsel said Fr Molloy was struck by Mr Flynn in a row over who was going to get the next drink.

Mr Groarke said it was up to the jury to determine what happened. Fr Molloy was alive at 9.45pm when he was enjoying the company of the Flynns, having visited their neighbour's house that evening, but was discovered injured and possibly dead by 1am the following morning.

Over the next three hours, the jury of 10 men and two women heard evidence from 14 prosecution witnesses.

The trial opened with evidence from Detective Garda Michael Campbell, from the Garda Technical Bureau, who confirmed finding an eight-and-a-half-foot long drag mark of what appeared to be blood in the master bedroom where Niall's body lay. There were also traces of blood on the newel post at the top of the stairs.

Next, Douglas Goodbody, a neighbour of the Flynns, who had attended the post-wedding luncheon on 7 July, took the stand. He knew the Flynns and Fr Molloy for around 15 years and they shared a mutual interest in horses, the court heard.

Fr Molloy, he said, was in "good humour" when he arrived at Kilcoursey House for lunch that Sunday.

The retired farmer further testified that the Flynns and Fr Molloy had called to his home at 7.30pm that evening and stayed for approximately two hours.

During this time they had about three drinks each, Fr Molloy taking gin and tonic and Mr and Mrs Flynn whiskey, and they inspected some horses before leaving at 9.20pm. Mr Goodbody said his guests were all in "very good humour and very friendly" when they left his home to return to Kilcoursey.

James Lowry, a young groom employed by the Flynns and Niall, then took the witness stand. Mr Lowry gave evidence that he attended a football match in Tullamore that Sunday and later that day saw Niall at Kilcoursey House, and the priest appeared to be in "good form". He also met Mrs Flynn in the house later that evening at 9pm.

Mr Lowry, however, said he then left the house and did not return until 3am when he was met by members of the Flynn family and learned of Fr Molloy's death. He remained in the house until 4am and later returned at 6.30am.

The first member of the Flynn family to give evidence was Maureen (Flynn) Parkes, a trained nurse whose wedding had taken place in Kilcoursey the day before Niall's death.

Maureen recalled that Fr Molloy and her parents visited the Goodbodys that Sunday and seemed in "good form" when they returned to Kilcoursey House at around 9.45pm that night.

She had left Kilcoursey that evening to join her husband and siblings in White's pub in the village before going back to her brother David's home, Tober House, at around midnight for coffee and sandwiches. She and her husband left Tober House at 1am and returned to Kilcoursey, where she found her father, Richard, in a distressed state.

Maureen told the court she went upstairs to her parents' bedroom and saw Fr Molloy lying on the floor just inside the door. Her mother, Therese, was kneeling beside him. Niall did not have a pulse when she checked and she then turned her attention to looking after her mother.

In evidence, parish priest Fr James Deignan recalled receiving a phone call from Richard Flynn at 1am that night. Mr Flynn requested that he come to Kilcoursey House immediately and be prepared to anoint someone.

Arriving at Kilcoursey, the local priest was brought upstairs to find a man lying on the floor but he did not recognise him at the time. "I wasn't sure whether he was alive or dead," Fr Deignan said, also confirming that he had administered the Last Rites.

The parish priest said he and Richard tried to phone Dr Daniel O'Sullivan, a local doctor in Kilbeggan, to no avail. "We were not successful at that moment and I asked Mr Flynn if we could try some other numbers of other doctors and he got me the phone book. I had forgotten to bring my glasses with me and this necessitated me going back to the parochial house to get my glasses," he told the court.

At that time, he was only aware of Mr and Mrs Flynn's presence in the house but when he returned minutes later, he found several people there. "I brushed past them in my anxiety to get in contact with a doctor as quickly as possible," he said.

Failing to get a doctor on the phone, Fr Deignan then drove to Kilbeggan, accompanied by one of the Flynn's daughters, Zandra, to alert Dr O'Sullivan, who returned with them.

Taking the witness stand, Dr O'Sullivan said he found Fr Molloy lying on the bedroom floor when he arrived at Kilcoursey at 2am that night.

"He was covered with a blanket or something when I went in and I didn't realise why he had died until I removed the blanket from his face," he said.

"He was still warm and there was no question of any rigor mortis having set in so I gather it was a relatively short time. That is all I can say," he added.

Dr O'Sullivan testified that Mrs Flynn, who was in the same room, was "quite hysterical" and was later taken to hospital. At no point did anyone consider calling an ambulance for Fr Molloy.

Sgt Kevin Forde from Clara Garda Station was the first police officer to arrive at the crime scene that night. He made his way to Kilcoursey after Fr Deignan had called to the station at 3.15am.

Arriving at the house, Sgt Forde observed the body of a fully dressed man lying on the floor of the master bedroom. The dead man was identified to him as Fr Niall Molloy.

On removing the towel from Fr Molloy's face, Sgt Forde observed a cut to the priest's upper lip, which was burst, and a cut to his lower left jaw. There was a large streak of blood on the white carpet and pooled blood at Fr Molloy's head, as well as blood stains and spatters elsewhere in the bedroom.

Sgt Forde told the court that the accused appeared to be unshaken by events. "I saw Richard Flynn sitting on a sofa in the (sitting) room. He was drinking a mug of coffee and he asked me to have one. He appeared very relaxed, cool and calm," he said.

The businessman apologised for calling the local sergeant out at that hour. "He said 'It's a messy old business', indicating the body upstairs. I started to caution him that he wasn't obliged to say anything, but he waved his hand and told me that he understood all that," Sgt Forde said.

Mr Flynn said an argument developed about who would go downstairs to get another drink and that he struck his wife with his left hand once and Fr Molloy with his right hand, at least twice. "That is all there is to it," the accused had told Sgt Forde.

The scene was preserved and Inspector Thomas Monaghan from Tullamore Garda Station arrived at 4.25am and was introduced to Richard. "On sitting down, Mr Flynn said 'I am the culprit'," Sgt Forde explained.

Mr Flynn told Gardaí that his wife and Fr Molloy were unconscious and he poured water over both of them in a bid to revive them.

"He then contacted Fr Deignan and tried to contact Dr O'Sullivan. When he had done that he came back upstairs and he found that Fr Molloy was dead and his wife was in a hysterical state in the room," Sgt Forde told the trial.

In evidence, Inspector Thomas Monaghan described the bedroom scene: "There was blood on the floor near the head and a large patch of blood similar to a drag mark between the body and the bed in the room, my lord, about five or six feet long and about seven or eight inches wide, my lord, on the white carpet."

Mr Flynn, he said, apologised "for the trouble" and for calling Gardaí out at such a late hour. "He took me and Sergeant Forde to a sitting room and on sitting down he said 'I am the culprit' and he apologised again for taking us out of bed," Inspector Monaghan said.

On cautioning Mr Flynn, Inspector Monaghan asked if he had found his wife and Fr Molloy in a "compromising position" to which the accused replied: "No, no. Nothing like that."

The Inspector said the accused indicated they had all consumed quite an amount of alcohol and that a "stupid argument" developed over getting another drink.

"He got out of bed to go down to get a drink for himself and that at that stage he was physically attacked by his wife and Fr Molloy because he indicated that he was not going to get drink for them," Inspector Monaghan said.

Mr Flynn told Gardaí he struck his wife once in the face with his fist and then struck Fr Molloy two to three times, causing both of them to fall to the floor.

Both were unconscious and Mr Flynn tried to revive them by pouring water on their faces. "He said his wife came around but he noticed that Fr Molloy was breathing with difficulty and that he knew he had a heart condition. He then ran downstairs and telephoned Fr Deignan and tried to contact Dr O'Sullivan but was unsuccessful," Inspector Monaghan told the court.

The court heard that Mr Flynn declined to sign Inspector Monaghan's interview notes when they were read back to him but gave a commitment to make a full statement the following day.

On 15 July 1985, one week after Niall's death, Richard's solicitor attended Tullamore Garda Station to provide a statement confirming that the interview notes were correct and a true account of what happened.

The court then heard evidence from Niall's brother, Billy Molloy, who immediately went to Kilcoursey House on hearing of his brother's death. There, he met Richard for the first time, who apologised for what had happened.

"Mr Flynn said again that he was terribly sorry for the whole thing and I said 'What happened?' and he said it was a political row, it started with a political row. Now there is one thing there, your honour, that you might say," Billy told the court before Judge Roe interrupted his testimony and Mr Groarke reminded him to stick to the questions asked.

The court heard that as Billy pressed Mr Flynn for answers, the long-time business associate and friend of Niall's grew agitated and uncomfortable. "He started scratching his face and I noticed under his fingernails, of the right hand, that all the blood was congealed and there was a swelling on the back of the right hand and I said, 'Is that the hand that killed my brother?'" Billy told the court, causing a close relative to collapse in tears in the courtroom.

Billy then confirmed that Mr Flynn broke down and became distressed when one of his daughters entered the sitting room offering coffee. He declined and left shortly afterwards.

Billy's evidence raised questions over what had happened on the night but other key witnesses never got to testify.

After breaking for lunch, State Pathologist Dr John Harbison took the stand to provide the results of his post-mortem on Niall's body.

The deceased, he said, was dressed in a blue pullover, collar-attached shirt, trousers, shoes and socks and there was a sports jacket on the floor close to the feet. There were male and female clothes scattered around the room and blood stains extending six feet from the bed to the door.

Dr Harbison gave evidence that Niall had lacerations to the left of his mouth, bruises on the nose and right cheekbone, grazing on the right ear and a laceration over the left lower jaw. Both knees and the left shin were bruised and there was an abrasion on the left thigh. There were also minor grazes on the tip of the chin as well as slight bruising on the left arm.

The State Pathologist said there was evidence of swelling and bleeding on the brain and that Fr Molloy's lungs were water-logged and three times the normal weight.

Blood and urine samples showed evidence of alcohol consumption but reflected normal social drinking, he said.

Dr Harbison concluded that the acute brain swelling was caused by multiple injuries to the head and neck, likely from five or six blows, probably by a fist.

He ruled out the possibility of acute heart failure as the cause of death, stating that the degree of heart disease was "minor" and about normal for a man of 52.

The jaw injury sustained by Fr Molloy, he said, was caused by something harder than a fist and a kick or a fall against a wall or furniture could not be ruled out.

There was no trace of defensive injuries or marks on Fr Molloy's body, indicating that the priest had not struck any blows or attempted to ward off blows, the court heard.

Under cross-examination by defence counsel Patrick McEntee SC, Dr Harbison conceded that he could not positively rule out the possibility of acute heart failure as the cause of death but he believed the head injuries sustained were the more likely cause.

The trial continued to hear forensic evidence from Gardaí and Dr Maureen Smyth, a forensic scientist with the Department of Justice.

The court heard Fr Molloy and Richard and Therese Flynn each had different blood groups and that stains consistent with blood from Niall and Therese were found on the accused's pyjama top. Mrs Flynn's night clothes also had blood matching Fr Molloy.

Blood stains found on the bedspread, duvet and carpet were consistent with Fr Molloy's blood; there was also one blood stain linked to Richard on the duvet.

Detective Garda Michael Keating told the court there was blood on the doors, wall and picture frames, on the wash hand basin, radiator, window ledge, bed covers, TV screen and on two magazines in the room.

And it was then that the trial came asunder. The jury was directed to leave the courtroom as legal submissions were made.

In the absence of the jury, Mr McEntee raised a doubt in the medical evidence and asked Judge Roe to direct the jury to give a 'not guilty' verdict on both charges.

Close to an hour of legal argument followed. Mr McEntee submitted that the possibility of acute heart failure as the cause of death could not be ruled out.

"He (Dr Harbison) cannot dispose of the possibility that death was due, having regard to the condition of the late Fr Molloy's heart, my lord, and it was diseased; he cannot dispose of the possibility that he, having become angry and exerted himself as a result of that anger and the statement of Mr Flynn establishes those facts, my lord, that his death or that the physiological process that ended in his death resulted from the heart condition and the excitement and acute heart failure rather than from the blows, my lord," Mr McEntee said.

He argued that all three parties were suffering from fatigue and alcohol consumption when the "foolish dispute" arose over drink and that Mr Flynn was acting in self-defence when he struck his wife and long-standing friend.

It was also possible, he submitted, that Fr Molloy fell against a hard object in the bedroom causing the injury to his jaw but there was an onus on the prosecution to prove that Mr Flynn used excessive force. "Certainly, it would be quite wrong for the jury to speculate that it was caused by a kick," Mr McEntee said.

The defence counsel further argued that it was a case of misadventure and that Mr Flynn did not intend to cause harm.

"This, my lord, in my respectful submission, is as near to an accident, to a pure accident, a pure unintended occurrence as one could find and again, my lord, if proof of that is needed further, my lord, you have only to look at the reaction of Mr Flynn after the incident," Mr McEntee said.

"This is a most sad, sad occurrence, my lord, but, in my respectful submission, an occurrence which is not criminal in any meaningful sense of that word," he added.

In response, Mr Groarke said a plea of misadventure was not open to the court and there was sufficient evidence to go to the jury.

Dr Harbison, he said, was satisfied that Niall's death had resulted from head injuries and not from a heart attack.

"He (Dr Harbison) stuck to his guns, my lord, that he was satisfied it was his opinion that the cause of death was the head injuries and that subdural haemorrhage which the deceased suffered from," Mr Groarke said.

Even if the assault had caused a heart attack, it did not exonerate Mr Flynn, he added.

On hearing both sides, Judge Roe said he had "no hesitation" in granting Mr McEntee's application.

The gravity of his ruling, however, did not become clear until the jury was called back just after 4.30pm.

It was then that Judge Roe dropped a bombshell and directed the 12 jury members to return a verdict of 'not guilty' on both charges because of a doubt over the medical evidence.

Explaining his ruling, Judge Roe said it was a "very sad case" from start to finish and that it was possible that Fr Molloy sustained injuries while falling to the ground or suffered a heart attack.

"In this case there is no evidence as to what happened except the statement made by Mr Flynn, and on his own statement it would not be proper to convict him on either count," Judge Roe said.

"The possibility of self-defence is undoubtedly brought into the picture by the evidence and if only two or three blows were struck it would be impossible to say that more force was used than was necessary," he added.

Judge Roe sympathised with both families, describing the case as a "great tragedy".

"It is perfectly clear from all the evidence that the friendship between Fr Molloy and Mrs Flynn was a perfectly proper one, so proper that he was in Mr and Mrs Flynn's bedroom. They were great friends for nearly 30 years and there is not an iota of evidence that there was anything improper in their relationship," Judge Roe said.

The trio had probably taken a little more drink than normal but nobody intended to cause harm, he said.

"This is not the first time that friends have struck each other blows, but in this case all parties were very unlucky in that the blows led to death. I have not the slightest doubt that Mr Flynn had not the remotest intention of killing Fr Molloy or of causing him any harm whatever and, as far as Mr Flynn is concerned, he must have suffered appalling mental agony since this unfortunate matter; it will live with him for the rest of his life," Judge Roe remarked.

"For these reasons, I think, whilst it is a little bit unusual, it is not improper for me to express sympathy with all parties over this dreadful matter. Nobody intended anything wrong to happen, any injury to be caused," he added.

Judge Roe's sensational direction to the jury to acquit Richard Flynn, without considering all of the evidence in the case, caused widespread shock and consternation.

For the families at the heart of the trial, it led to tears on both sides – tears of joy and relief for Richard and his family; tears of anguish and devastation for the Molloys and the parish of Castlecoote.

Throughout the four-hour trial, Richard showed little sign of emotion. When Judge Roe ruled, he gave a slight smile and shook hands with his defence team before walking out of court a free man.

While the businessman refused to talk to reporters, his daughter, Maureen, simply said: "We are very happy."

The Molloy family, however, were left stunned. Billy broke down as he left the courthouse and remarked there was no justice in Ireland.

Dissatisfied with the verdict, Billy told the *Irish Times* after the trial: "I'm going to the American Embassy to renew my passport and I won't be coming back."

The national newspaper also reported at the time that the direction by Judge Roe was unusual in the circuit court and only occurred in around one in five cases, according to legal sources.

A week later, Billy told a local paper, the *Westmeath Independent*, that the trial was a "shambles" and vowed to campaign for the outcome to be redressed. "I'm going to start this all over again. All I want is the truth."

The shock of Richard Flynn's acquittal rippled far beyond the Molloy family, causing deep unease in wider society and within political circles.

Judge Roe came under pressure to explain his actions. The Director of Public Prosecutions, Eamon Barnes, deflected criticism that his Office had not done its job. The then Minister for Justice Alan Dukes refused to meet with the Molloy family in the wake of the shock trial verdict and suggested any meeting would be "improper" when a full inquest was pending.

There were also claims of interference from the Church in the Molloy case.

Within a week of the trial, Fine Gael TD Liam Skelly claimed, under Dáil privilege, that Cardinal Tomás Ó Fiaich and other senior church figures had intervened in the case.

During a debate on legislation on 'Malicious Injuries', Deputy Skelly said: "Questions arise with regard to the slowness in having the defendant arrested, why three months elapsed before there was an arrest. Indeed, questions arise as to why it was necessary for the Cardinal and the local Bishop of Elphin to become involved."

Drawing on another contentious case in 1984, in which a gay man died following an assault in a public park in Dublin, Deputy Skelly said: "One might well pose the question: is there now a new rule which says it is all right to beat a person to death as long as it is in a public park at night time or in a bedroom? Is that the proposition put to citizens as a result of the decision in this case? Questions will continue to arise about this case. Indeed, they will continue to be asked in this House until such time as they are answered satisfactorily.

"The Church and Cardinal must answer for their interference in this case. We must all know why it was necessary to have this interference, why it is that people are so anxious to hush up the facts of this case."

The Church refuted any claims of interference. In a statement, Cardinal Ó Fiaich, Bishop of Elphin Dominic Conway, and Auxiliary Bishop for Meath, Michael Smith, said the allegations were without foundation and should be withdrawn if not substantiated.

The Dublin West TD, however, said his confidential sources were very reliable. "The bishops will know whether or not they have interfered. The local people will know whether or not they interfered, and the whole country is buzzing with talk and dissatisfaction with the happenings in this case," he told the *Irish Press*.

The following week, Deputy Skelly attempted to raise the issue again when he alleged that the establishment were covering up events in the Molloy case. His efforts led to the Dáil being adjourned twice.

"The Government do not want democracy to prevail," Deputy Skelly said. "I cannot raise a legitimate matter like the death of Fr Molloy in this House because the establishment and everybody else are playing cards together and want it covered up and smothered. They are succeeding in doing so. I will try to raise it again. It is a disgrace. As a Member of Parliament I am ashamed of this action. The circumstances under which this man died have been covered up."

The Fine Gael TD also criticised the Office of the DPP for its handling of the Molloy case, which was met with a swift rebuttal from its Director, Eamon Barnes, who said his Office discharged its duty in the case with "scrupulous care". Even with the benefit of hindsight, Mr Barnes said, it was clear that there was nothing that should have been done by his Office which was not done.

Within days, Deputy Skelly was joined by Dáil colleagues Liam Naughten, Bernard Allen, Proinsias De Rossa and Michael Keating in calling for an inquiry into the handling of the Molloy case.

"I am only trying to say in the Houses of Parliament what every person in the country is saying — that there are a lot of unanswered questions about the case," Deputy Skelly said.

Speaking in the Dáil, Deputy Allen said there appeared to be "one law for the rich and one law for the poor" and called for an independent body to monitor the performance of judges.

Workers Party TD Proinsias De Rossa sought legislative changes preventing a judge from dismissing serious charges before going to a jury, while Progressive Democrat TD Michael Keating asked for legislation to be reviewed to ensure that court decisions could be more fully explained.

In the Dáil, Roscommon TD Terry Leyden asked whether the trial result should be referred to the Supreme Court under the Criminal Procedure Act 1967 but was ruled out of order. He then questioned the timing of the inquest after the criminal trial but any concerns were quickly dismissed by the Minister for Justice.

"I would not find it at all unusual that the inquest is taking place following the court case to which the Deputy has referred, because an inquest cannot be held when criminal proceedings are pending. There is no significance whatever to be attached to the timing in this case," Minister Alan Dukes said.

The Justice Minister also resisted calls for a public inquiry, stressing that all facts in the case would be examined at an inquest to take place in a matter of weeks.

Minister Dukes said: "I have been authoritatively informed that arrangements are in train to have an inquest held in this case. The date is already fixed, at least tentatively, for 24 July."

As political pressure continued to mount, the Molloy family spoke of their shock and disappointment over the troubling trial result.

The family contemplated taking a private prosecution for murder against Richard Flynn and set up a "fighting fund" to support their cause, which drew widespread support from across the country.

They were particularly concerned over the fact that Fr Molloy may have been owed money by the Flynns and that he wished to disentangle himself from his business dealings with Therese before his death – something that was never addressed during the trial.

Speaking to RTE's current affairs programme *Today Tonight*, the family raised concern that money and business dealings may have been at the heart of events that night.

Fr Molloy's nephew, Ian Maher, told the TV programme that his uncle had been depressed days before his death over a land deal in which he had paid up to IR£12,000 to the Flynns.

"Up to the Thursday before his death, the money had not been repaid. Niall was recorded as saying that. I think it agitated him because the man appeared depressed for some days before he was killed," Mr Maher said.

The deposit related to lands at Kilcoursey House but the land deal never went ahead.

"The element of trust in the Flynns was long – over 28 years – and was badly shaken over this particular deal. I know he had been advised to extricate his finances from the whole set-up. Certainly, I know it caused him considerable concern but I am sure it was more because of what he considered a betrayal of friendship than the fiscal aspects of it," Mr Maher said.

Fr Molloy's nephew also questioned why evidence of a row downstairs in the house was not presented in court: "I was amazed that this was not brought out."

The Book of Evidence had detailed the land deal and money as a possible motive in Niall's death. Despite Gardaí having knowledge of this critical aspect, key witnesses were never called to give evidence and it was never raised or probed at Richard's trial.

As the first anniversary of Fr Molloy's death drew close that July, the Justice Minister reiterated his view that the upcoming inquest would deal with all of the facts.

"I do not think we are over-emphasising this or over-stressing it to say that it is the occasion when any relevant information can and should be brought forward. I am as concerned, I will not say more than most, but I am concerned as much to establish the facts and circumstances of this case in the proper manner," Minister Dukes said.

Today, more than three decades on, Mr Dukes, who is no longer in public office, admits that Judge Roe's controversial ruling continues to beg questions.

"I think like everybody else I was surprised that the judge in the case so quickly directed the jury to return a verdict of not guilty. That surprised me, I must say, I couldn't understand it and I think to this day it's very difficult to look behind the reasons why that direction would have been given at the time," he told the recent RTE documentary *The Killing of Fr Niall Molloy...*

At Fr Molloy's first anniversary Mass, children from the local equestrian club founded by the keen horseman formed a guard of honour outside the church in Castlecoote, where family, friends and parishioners gathered to remember him.

With the inquest just weeks away, Billy Molloy held out hope that the truth would finally emerge, telling one national newspaper: "That will be our day."

Chapter 3
A HARD WON VERDICT

In the wake of the shock trial result, all eyes turned to the inquest into Fr Niall Molloy's death.

Scheduled to open on 24 July 1986, the Justice Minister Alan Dukes came under pressure to release the Garda investigation file to the Molloy family.

The family had pertinent questions over the bloody drag mark in the bedroom, the orderly position of Niall's body and the time lag between the alleged row and initial contact with Gardaí. There were questions too over broken furniture and suggestions of an altercation downstairs and the evidential value of the cleric's watch, which was damaged and had stopped working at 10.40.

Three days before the inquest into Fr Molloy's death was due to open, Richard and Therese Flynn's solicitor, Liam Lysaght, wrote to the Attorney General, Minister for Justice and Garda Commissioner objecting to the Garda investigation file being made available to the Molloy family.

Mr Lysaght registered "the strongest possible objection" to material being furnished to the Molloy family or anyone else.

"A Garda investigation file, of its nature, almost certainly contains irrelevant, interpretative and speculative material. Such material would undoubtedly be used, we fear, to further the campaign from which our clients have so grievously and unjustly suffered," he wrote.

He also advised that both Richard and Therese had been "subjected to a sustained campaign of comment in the media, much of which has been speculative and hurtful to each of them".

At the eleventh hour, Minister Dukes released part of the investigation file to the Molloy family.

Some last-minute decisions also saw the State and Attorney General being represented at the inquest by Seamus McKenna, a formidable senior counsel, accompanied by junior counsel Hugh Hartnett.

The county coroner, Dr Patrick Grealy, was replaced by his deputy due to a bout of laryngitis. Presiding over the inquest was local solicitor and Deputy Coroner for County Offaly, Brian Mahon, a son of District Court Judge Seamus Mahon.

Appearing for the Flynn family was Mr James Connolly BL, while Mr Peter Charleton BL represented the Molloy family. Fr Deignan also had his own legal representation.

This was the Molloy family's second bid for the truth, as they put their faith in the inquest shedding light on the events on that summer Sunday.

And so the scene was set for the inquest to establish how, when and where Niall died.

DAY ONE: THURSDAY, 24 JULY 1986.

The inquest opened in Tullamore with a cautionary note, as the

Deputy Coroner Brian Mahon highlighted the limitations of Section 30 of the Coroners Act.

"There may well be another forum in another court where questions of wmotive or background matter may correctly be adduced, but it is not at this inquiry and to avoid any breach of the law or miscarriage of justice where the verdict of this inquest could be quashed or called into question, I would ask you gentlemen to bear all of this in mind in your examination or cross-examination," Mr Mahon said.

The first witness was State Pathologist Dr John Harbison, who outlined in great detail what he found when he was called to Kilcoursey House on the morning of 8 July, one year previously.

Fr Molloy's body, bloodied and battered, lay just inside the doorway of the large double bedroom, which was in a state of "slight disorder". There was a double wardrobe, dressing table, rocking chair, two bedside lockers, a TV on a bedside locker, and a record player.

Describing the room, Dr Harbison said it was not in any great state of disorder apart from where male and female clothes were scattered around the bed, floor and chairs. No furniture had been overturned.

Fr Molloy was lying on his back and dressed in a blue round-necked jumper, a collared blue shirt, dark grey trousers, shoes and socks. A brown herringbone tweed sports jacket lay on the floor beside his feet.

On removing a rust-coloured towel covering Niall's face, Dr Harbison observed a white froth coming from the dead priest's mouth, an injury to his left upper lip, as well as an injury to his left cheek.

"There was blood staining of the thick carpet on the floor over a distance of eight foot to nine foot," he told the inquest.

"That staining nearest to the deceased was dark and appeared to have been due to direct bleeding onto the surface, that is the surface of the carpet, but the remainder was fainter and suggested a smear or wipe," Dr Harbison added.

Fr Molloy's body was taken to Tullamore Hospital, where the State Pathologist carried out a post-mortem examination. Before this started, Dr Daniel O'Sullivan, the Flynn family GP who attended Kilcoursey on the night, paid the State Pathologist a visit, although it is unclear what was discussed or said at this time. Dr O'Sullivan had also treated Niall on occasion, the inquest heard.

Continuing his evidence, Dr Harbison told the inquest that he removed a wrist watch and gold miraculous medal and chain from Fr Molloy's body. Other personal possessions included IR£115 in bank notes and two sets of Toyota car keys.

Detailing the injuries sustained, he said the deceased had several lacerations or irregular cuts to his face and head, as well as cuts to the thigh and ankle. The body also showed faded bruising to the arm, knees and shin area.

He further told the inquest that he examined samples of Fr Molloy's brain tissue on 30 July 1985, alongside a medical colleague who was a specialist in neuropathology.

Summarising his findings, Dr Harbison said: "I came to the conclusion that Fr Niall Molloy died of acute brain swelling and acute subdural haemorrhage both resulting from multiple injuries to the head and neck, principally to the face. The distribution of those injuries is consistent with the deceased being the recipient of five or six or even more blows, eg by a fist. The violence was insufficient to fracture any facial bones or for that matter to break any teeth."

He added there was evidence of 'cerebral lung' as a result of the head injuries sustained, which caused fluid to accumulate or the water-logging of Niall's lungs. This had given rise to the white froth observed coming from his mouth. The priest was also found to have a "slightly enlarged heart".

"No injury of a defensive or offensive nature was present on the arms or hands," he told the inquest.

An analysis of blood and urine suggested that Fr Molloy was above the drink-driving limit at the time (100mg per 100mls blood) but was not drunk.

The amount of alcohol detected was "within the limits of ordinary social drinking" at 134.7mg / 100mls blood and 196.6mg / 100mls urine. "I would not say he was drunk at that time," the State Pathologist said, further explaining that the blood and urine test results suggested that alcohol had been consumed "over quite a period of time prior to death".

The cause of death, Dr Harbison concluded, was acute brain swelling and acute subdural haemorrhage due to head injuries. He firmly ruled out heart failure: "No evidence of recent infarction was noted."

The time of death, the State Pathologist estimated, was between 11pm on 7 July and 5am the following morning but he could not say which side of midnight Niall had died.

Under cross-examination by Peter Charleton for the Molloy family, Dr Harbison said he could not really say how long it took Niall to die. "Death from brain swelling can occur in a few minutes, subdural haemorrhage is slower and takes longer," he said.

Medical intervention and hospital treatment, he said, may have improved Fr Molloy's chances of survival. "This is always speculative. He would certainly have had a better chance," he added.

Under cross-examination by counsel for the Flynns, Dr Harbison said it was possible that Fr Molloy struck a hard object in the bedroom, such as the bedpost or the corner of a nearby table, but said the forensic evidence did not support that theory.

"Where someone falls and cuts the skin they shed some of their blood and that was absent. ... There tends to be a trace of blood at that impact point. That was not here," he said.

He further ruled out the possibility that Fr Molloy could have died from inhaling vomit to his lungs.

The inquest then heard a counter argument to Dr Harbison's findings, when pathologist Dr John Gilsenan appeared on behalf of the Flynns.

Dr Gilsenan, who worked at hospitals in Portlaoise and Tullamore, submitted that Fr Molloy died from pulmonary oedema or the water-logging of his lungs, which may have been caused by one of three events – arrhythmia or an irregular heart-beat, head injury, or choking on vomit.

His conclusions were drawn from an assessment of heart and brain tissue samples and not on a post-mortem or any examination of the body.

It was possible, he suggested, that Fr Molloy suffered heart failure by losing his temper during a violent struggle. He also questioned how the State Pathologist could single out head injury as the cause of the water-logging on the priest's lungs and ultimately his death.

In cross-examination, Mr Charleton challenged the theory put forward by Dr Gilsenan: "What you are suggesting is that Fr Molloy flies into a temper and there is no evidence of that; he gets heart failure; he is hit five or six times to his head – the injuries to the brain resulting but they are absolutely nothing to do with the cause of death because he was going to die anyway, is that what you are saying?"

Mr Gilsenan replied: "It is a possibility. I am saying there are three possible reasons why he got pulmonary oedema."

Recalled to the witness stand, Dr Harbison disputed the counter-argument offered by Dr Gilsenan.

Forensic evidence focusing on Fr Molloy's watch and broken furniture found in Kilcoursey House after the weekend of wedding celebrations brought the first day of the inquest to a close.

Members of the Garda Technical Bureau – Garda Anthony Byrne, Detective Garda Michael Campbell, Detective Sergeant Edwin Handcock, Detective Garda Oliver Cloonan, and Detective Garda Declan Buckley – gave evidence of preserving the bedroom scene and collecting samples for forensic analysis.

Garda Buckley and Garda Cloonan further testified that Fr Molloy's watch was working at the post-mortem, despite not handling it directly. The State Pathologist, they added, had remarked that the watch was working during a conversation about the Air India disaster off the Cork coast, just weeks earlier in June 1985. Their statements about the watch were made a year following Fr Molloy's death, after the priest's family raised the watch as an issue of concern in a *Today Tonight* TV programme.

Detective Sergeant Handcock then detailed his findings from an examination of the broken furniture discovered downstairs at Kilcoursey House. This included a large three-legged oval table in the dining room, with a missing brass claw foot, and a broken coffee table in the TV room.

"One of the feet was broken off the leg nearest the fireplace and a piece of folded cardboard had been placed beneath it for support. The broken piece of wood was lying on the mantelpiece of the fireplace," he explained.

After examining the broken bamboo and glass coffee table in the TV room, the Detective Sergeant found missing fragments of glass from the table top in a trailer to the rear of the house. No traces of blood were found in the TV room or in any of the downstairs rooms, he said.

The technical evidence continued with Dr Maureen Smyth, a forensic scientist at the national Forensic Science Laboratory, detailing the samples received from Gardaí for analysis.

Samples included swabs from blood stains in the bedroom and the stair banister, as well as blood samples from the parties involved, namely Fr Molloy and Therese and Richard Flynn.

Among other samples listed were bloodstained carpet fibres, night clothes from Richard and Therese, Fr Molloy's clothing, clothing from the bedroom floor, bedclothes, a bloodstained magazine, a piece of leaf labelled as 'debris from neck of Fr Niall Molloy', and a green button with thread and fabric attached.

Richard was wearing green pyjamas on the night while Therese's night clothes were handed over from Tullamore Hospital on the Monday morning after Fr Molloy's death.

Gardaí also took samples from what was believed to be Fr Molloy's bedroom, including a glass of milk, a cigar end from an ashtray, and a Pikeur cigar and box with three half Corona cigars.

Dr Smyth then explained how blood samples from the Flynns and Fr Molloy were analysed and grouped – each was found to have a distinct blood group, which made them distinguishable from each other.

"A number of bloodstains on the pyjama top were consistent with the blood of Niall Molloy. I fully grouped a stain on the front and found it matched the blood of Niall Molloy, containing a combination of groups present in approximately three persons in every thousand of the population. A bloodstain on the left back matched the blood of Therese Flynn containing a combination of groups present in approximately one person in every thousand of the population. I grouped two stains on the pyjama bottom and both these matched Richard Flynn's own blood," Dr Smyth said.

"The pyjama jacket was ripped under the left arm and the top button had been ripped out," she added, pointing out that the missing button had been found elsewhere in the bedroom.

The forensic scientists also found that blood stains on Therese's nightdress and dressing gown was consistent with that of Fr Molloy.

Niall's blood was found on the sweater and trousers he was wearing, while a small stain over the pocket on the back of his trousers was consistent with Richard's blood, the inquest heard.

Blood swabs taken from around the bedroom were consistent with the priest's blood, except for one stain on the duvet, which was consistent with Richard's blood group.

Blood on a yellow towel from the bathroom opposite the master bedroom was ruled out as Niall's and may have come from either Richard or Therese.

Swabs taken from some blood stains could not be grouped, such as a stain found on the newel post at the top of the stairs in Kilcoursey House.

While this forensic evidence was presented at the inquest, it was not given any context or meaning in relation to how Fr Molloy died. There was no explanation as to why some blood stains could not be grouped.

It is worth bearing in mind that in 1985, the analysis of blood samples was limited to blood grouping, as advances in DNA technology and sequencing had yet to be developed or applied to criminal casework.

DNA was only used for the first time in a criminal case in 1987 in the UK and in 1994 in Ireland.

DAY TWO: FRIDAY, 25 JULY 1986.

After a day of forensic and medical evidence, the second day of the inquest hoped to shed new light on events in Kilcoursey House on the night of Fr Molloy's death.

For the first time, Therese Flynn was expected to break her silence and the expectations of finally getting to the truth were high.

On the day, however, Richard and Therese suffered from memory lapses that only compounded the growing unease and sense of frustration surrounding the unexplained death.

The inquest resumed with further evidence from Garda Michael Fox and Detective Garda Michael Keating in relation to Fr Molloy's watch, which had become a contentious issue since the trial, just weeks earlier.

In a supplementary statement, Garda Michael Fox, who escorted Fr Molloy's body to the morgue in Tullamore, said he took possession of the dead priest's personal effects, including his watch, at the post-mortem. He noticed the glass on the face of the watch was broken but still in place and he did not recall if the watch had stopped or what time was on it.

Detective Garda Michael Keating, from the Garda Technical Bureau, gave further evidence of finding traces of blood on the top newel of the main staircase in the Flynns' home and also around the master bedroom where Fr Molloy lay dead. Traces of blood on the bedroom door were not identified.

The forensic evidence, he said, suggested that Niall's body was dragged across the carpet and that he was flipped over onto his back.

Blood found on the bed board was consistent with a bleeding hand touching it, he added.

In supplementary statements about Fr Molloy's watch, the Detective Garda said it was in working order when Dr Harbison passed it to him during the post-mortem and they had discussed how watches were found to be working after the Air India disaster.

Next to give evidence was Sergeant Kevin Forde, who was the first police officer to arrive at Kilcoursey House, after the local parish priest, Fr Jim Deignan, alerted him to the body of a dead man.

"He told me that the dead man was a priest whom he did not know and that he understood that he had fallen against a wall and hit his head," Sgt Forde recounted.

"He also stated that this was a terrible scandal in the parish and if there was any way in which it could be kept quiet. I told him that the death would have to be investigated and he then told me that when he was called to the Flynn home to administer the Last Rites, Richard Flynn had told him 'I'm the culprit'," Sgt Forde continued.

He immediately notified Tullamore Garda Station of the incident before making his way to Kilcoursey, where, at around

3.30am, he was shown to Fr Molloy's body upstairs by a local GP, Dr Daniel O'Sullivan.

Sgt Forde noted the wounds sustained by the dead priest, as well as the bloody drag mark on the carpet and blood stains elsewhere around the room.

The local sergeant then spoke to Richard, who was seated on a couch downstairs with a mug of coffee in one hand and his other arm stretched along the back of the settee. "He appeared to me to be calm and cool and unconcerned," he said.

Sgt Forde repeated his evidence, given at the criminal trial one month earlier, that Richard admitted to being the "culprit", having struck his wife and Niall and knocking them both unconscious.

In his supplementary statement, Sgt Forde said he took possession of Fr Molloy's watch, which was among the personal belongings handed over to Billy Molloy days after his death.

The glass on the watch, he said, was broken: "I noticed that the glass on the face of it was broken but still in place. I did not notice if the watch had stopped or what time was on it."

Among the other items handed over to the Molloy family were Niall's Toyota Carina car, a church collection of 97 envelopes of cash, two envelopes of money for Masses, a shotgun and a bunch of keys.

Detective Garda Noel Lynagh told the inquest that he had a conversation with Richard at Kilcoursey House in the early hours of 8 July. It was 5.30am when he observed that the businessman had bruises on the end joints of his right index finger and right thumbnail.

Agreeing that the bruises were as a result of striking Fr Molloy, Richard told Gda Lynagh, "I hit him under the chin, I know I did", as he made an upwards striking motion with his clenched fist.

The Detective Garda also noticed two small fresh-looking but clean scratches on the edge of Mr Flynn's left hand.

Richard, he said, seemed to be in a "distressed state of mind", adding that he made a formal request for the clothes Mr Flynn was wearing that night.

Gda Lynagh also said he understood that an elderly person, Auntie May, was present at the house at the time but that he did not see her.

The Garda evidence continued, with Detective Garda Sergeant John Dunne recounting his interview with Therese Flynn at Tullamore General Hospital on Tuesday, 9 July, where he found her to be "composed and lucid".

Mrs Flynn told him she had gone to bed early as she was tired and then remembered waking up to see her husband, Richard, and Fr Molloy chatting in the bedroom.

"She then recalled seeing Fr Molloy lying on the floor of the bedroom, she felt his arm for a pulse but could not find it, she gave him the kiss of life and that was all she could recall," he said.

The interview was relaxed and courteous, nothing contentious arose, and as the Gardaí left Therese remarked to her sister, "They were very nice."

Bringing the Garda evidence to a close, Inspector Tom Monaghan from Tullamore Garda Station, who interviewed Richard for 20 minutes on the night of Niall's death, described his observations at the time.

Mr Flynn told him that what happened arose from a "stupid argument" over who would go downstairs to get the next drink.

The businessman declined to sign the Inspector's notes despite confirming they were correct but committed to making a full statement the following day. When Inspector Monaghan returned, however, the family solicitor, Liam Lysaght, advised that Mr Flynn would not be making a statement but confirmed the facts already given.

Inspector Monaghan further told Mr Charleton, representing the Molloy family, that he did not interview members of the Flynn family after 8 July. "They declined to be interviewed by the Gardaí until their solicitor was present and they stated that they obtained legal advice to that effect," Inspector Monaghan said, adding that he later met Mr Lysaght, the family solicitor, who confirmed this and subsequently handed in prepared statements.

Additional statements by Inspector Monaghan relating to subsequent interviews and possible motive were excluded without challenge at the inquest.

The coroner explained: "It seems to me to be evidence of background or evidence of motive and the only logical reason to adduce this evidence would be to try to establish criminal liability or civil liability so I am not admitting it as a deposition to this inquest."

The inquest then turned to other witnesses who were present at Kilcoursey House on the night Fr Molloy died.

When Kilbeggan-based GP Dr Daniel O'Sullivan, who pronounced Niall dead at the scene, took the stand, he repeated his evidence of being called to Kilcoursey House at about 2am.

"I examined the man and found him to be dead. I did not move or disturb him in any way," the Flynn family doctor said.

"I also found Mrs Therese Flynn lying on the bedroom floor in a state of hysteria being attended to by her daughters Maureen and Anita. I gave her some treatment and admitted her to Tullamore General Hospital in my own car. I advised Fr Deignan to notify the Garda in Clara of the matter. Fr Molloy's body was quite warm and he appeared to be only dead a short time," he added.

Dr O'Sullivan also confirmed taking blood samples from the Flynns a week later on 15 July 1985.

When questioned under cross-examination, the doctor's testimony provided some insight into events on the night, although some of it jarred with evidence from other witnesses.

Responding to Mr Charleton, Dr O'Sullivan said he could not be exact about the time he arrived at Tullamore Hospital with Therese but denied it was before 2am and suggested it was closer to 3am that morning.

"An hour must have gone by from the time I arrived at Kilcoursey at about 2am and I was a long time treating Mrs Flynn and discussing what to do about her and that sort of thing, and it was a slow drive to the hospital. I would think, on the face of it, it was 3am when we got to the hospital," Dr O'Sullivan said.

When asked why he had not called an ambulance before arriving at the house, the local doctor said he was told the man, Fr Molloy, was dead. "I believed from Fr Deignan that he was dead and I rushed into the car and went on, which is what someone would normally do," he said.

Asked why he did not call the Gardaí before arriving at Kilcoursey, Dr O'Sullivan said: "I would never do that. I got a call to go to the house and I didn't know whether he was dead – I understood he was and I said I would go straight there and that is what one would normally do at that time of the night".

The GP said he asked Fr Deignan to alert the Gardaí as he left Kilcoursey with Mrs Flynn.

On the night, he had been woken up by Fr Deignan and Zandra Flynn and he denied telling a member of the Molloy family that it was David Flynn at the door that night.

On his way to Kilcoursey, the family doctor was unaware of any violence and understood that Fr Molloy had died naturally. "There was no mention whatsoever of that. They just said he was dead. I assumed he had died from natural causes," Dr O'Sullivan told the inquest.

"When I removed the cloth that was across his face I saw the marks on his face and the cut under his chin so I knew then that something had happened and I asked what happened," he said, adding that he did not notice any blood around the bedroom despite Garda evidence of a long bloody drag mark and blood stains around the room.

Dr O'Sullivan said he spent a considerable amount of time tending to Mrs Flynn, who was hysterical and appeared to be in a delusionary state.

"She became very violent and had to be physically restrained. It took two to three of us to keep her down. She struck out right, left and centre. I don't know how long it took," he said, adding that he gave "treatment" after a while.

"During this time she wanted to know was he really dead and she didn't believe it for some time. Most of my time was occupied with Mrs Flynn. I must say she gradually got a bit disorientated and somehow or other, before I took her away, she thought she had been in an accident with a horse," he added.

"As I took her into the car the last thing she said was 'look after the horses'. She was totally disorientated. She had a bruise as well on the left cheek. At one stage in the house when she became delirious I thought she was suffering from concussion and I thought it was better to take her to hospital," Dr O'Sullivan said, adding that it was his decision to take Mrs Flynn to hospital.

The family doctor said Therese was not drunk in the ordinary sense of the word nor was her husband, who appeared calm, despite events. "There was a good deal of panic among the family but he was pretty calm. He sort of expressed regret that this awful thing should happen," he told the inqŝuest.

Dr O'Sullivan was adamant that Richard told him there had been an argument downstairs, which he had assumed had later led to matters being 'thrashed out' in the bedroom.

Another drink was suggested and Therese said her husband could go down himself.

"She said 'you go down', that is speaking to Richard. He said there were some further words and they both suddenly attacked him physically. He said he lost his head and lashed out at both of them. He said Therese was knocked out. Fr Molloy, they were both knocked down," Dr O'Sullivan said.

"Fr Molloy got up and he struck him again. He said he might have given him three blows," he continued.

"Fr Molloy failed to get up. He didn't move. He appeared to be unconscious and he said he poured water on both their faces. Mrs Flynn revived but Fr Molloy didn't. I can't remember what else he said after that," he added.

He further told counsel for the Flynn family that he had "very little doubt" that Richard indicated there had been an argument downstairs that night: "I got the impression they had an argument downstairs first and he didn't tell me what the argument was about."

The inquest then heard from Dr Peter Greally, a doctor at Tullamore General Hospital, who attended to Therese in the early hours of 8 July. He met Mrs Flynn between 3.15am and 3.30am on the morning in question and referred her to a surgical colleague. He had previously told Gardaí it may have been between midnight and 2am but had since checked his notes.

Fr Deignan, the local parish priest, then took the stand.

Perhaps being overcautious following evidence that he asked the local sergeant for the matter to be kept quiet, Fr Deignan had legal representation at the inquest.

He detailed how Richard summoned him to Kilcoursey House at around 1am that night. "I went there immediately and was admitted to the house by Richard Flynn. Mr Flynn showed me upstairs to a room where I saw a man lying on his back on the floor. I administered the Last Rites to the man. I cannot say whether the man was dead or alive and I did not know who he was at that stage," Fr Deignan told the inquest.

"I noticed some blood stains on the carpet nearby. When I finished administering the Last Rites I went downstairs where I assisted Richard Flynn to telephone for a doctor," Fr Deignan added.

Having failed to get a doctor on the phone, however, he accompanied Zandra to Kilbeggan to call on Dr O'Sullivan. He further reiterated his previous evidence of returning to the parochial house for his glasses.

Fr Deignan told the Molloy family's counsel that he did not think to call Gardaí or an ambulance on the night. "I went there to do my own business as a priest," Fr Deignan said.

Incredibly, despite seeking medical attention, the parish priest said he did not call 999 because he was unaware that calling the emergency number would secure a doctor.

Instead, he said, they were trying to call local medics but he did not know the number of the nearest doctor, Dr Corboy, who lived in Clara village, just minutes away.

"I did not know his number at that particular time and I was anxious to help out the Flynn household," Fr Deignan said, adding it never crossed his mind to visit the doctor's home when he returned to the parochial house for his glasses.

He later clarified that one of the Flynn children discovered that Dr Corboy was away on that particular night and that other individuals had made the phone calls and not him.

Fr Deignan told the State's counsel that it was around 1.20am when he anointed Fr Molloy and that this took around five minutes. Therese was kneeling in the bedroom but did not say anything.

The parish priest did not ask any questions about what had happened and no information was volunteered, the inquest heard. He did not learn who the deceased was until he returned to the house when the Flynn children were present.

He accepted he was in the house for approximately two hours before Gardaí were alerted to the death at Kilcoursey. "There was a lot of confusion at the house and inevitably spending a lot of time in the kitchen talking to members of the family," he explained.

Fr Deignan said he had a conversation with Richard but could not divulge what was said because of his vocation: "I am sorry. I would not be able to assist the inquiry any further in that."

"I was there simply and solely as a priest to do my own business," he added.

He had no recollection of telling Sergeant Forde that the priest who was dead at Kilcoursey had fallen against a wall and struck his head. He could also not recall discussing the possible impact of the death on the local parish with the local sergeant.

The inquest then turned to members of the Flynn family, beginning with Miss May Quinn or Auntie May, an elderly relative living at Kilcoursey House, who was present in the house on the night.

In her deposition, Miss Quinn said: "When Therese, Richard and Fr Molloy came back to Kilcoursey from Goodbodys' there was no-one else in the house. We were in the drawing room; they were talking while I played Patience".

"Therese, Richard and Fr Molloy left the drawing room. Therese and Richard were tired and had said that they were going to bed," she added.

"I went out into the kitchen to get a glass of orange. I heard someone come in and went out into the hallway where I met Fr Molloy. He got himself a drink and went upstairs. I followed up in a few minutes," the statement continued.

Miss Quinn said she was not sleeping in her usual room but slept in the last room at the end of the corridor. "I did not hear anything else that night. I think it was about 12 o'clock when I went to bed," she said, adding that she did not learn of Fr Molloy's death until the next morning.

Under cross-examination, she said there was no argument of any description downstairs that night.

Next to take the stand was Maureen (Flynn) Parkes.

Reading a statement, given one week after Niall's death, into the record, the trained nurse said her wedding day "went off perfectly" and was followed by a cold buffet lunch the next day for family and friends.

The lunch began after 3pm and guests left at around 5pm. She remained at the house with her sister-in-law, Ann, while her parents and Fr Molloy went to visit the Goodbodys.

On their return to Kilcoursey at around 9.45pm, Maureen and Ann went to the pub to join their husbands Ralph and David, and her sisters, Anita and Zandra.

Afterwards, they returned to David's home at Tober for coffee and sandwiches before leaving for Kilcoursey House with their friends, Marie and Denis Hoctor, who intended to stay there that night.

The group arrived at Kilcoursey at 1am, where they met her father, Richard, who explained what happened.

"I went upstairs to my parents' bedroom. Fr Molloy was lying lengthways along the wall with his head towards the door and his feet towards the window. My mother was kneeling beside him trying to resuscitate him. He had a cut on the left side of his chin," Maureen said.

"I felt his right hand for a pulse but felt none. I closed his eyes. I covered his face with a towel. I put his arm over his chest," she added.

Maureen said she then turned to her mother who was "hysterical" and bruised on the jaw. "I hit her on the face. She appeared to pass out. When she revived, I put her head between her knees. She was hysterical again. I had to hold her arms with all my strength," she said.

Her mother was then sedated by the family doctor, who had since arrived at the house, and together with her sister, Anita, they brought Therese to Tullamore Hospital for medical attention. She was admitted at around 3am.

Anita stayed at the hospital, while Maureen returned to Kilcoursey House. "I went back to the hospital at about 8am. My mother was then in intensive care. She was waking every five minutes, would go into a panic, but when she saw me, she snapped back. Her voice was gone," Maureen said.

"Dr Durkan came and saw my mother and I told him of the bruising I had caused to her arms and the slap I had given to her face. He examined her thoroughly," she said, adding that she gave permission for her mother to be seen by a psychiatrist.

There were no questions from counsel for the Molloy family or the State.

Minutes later, a much-anticipated moment came in the inquest when Therese took the stand. Reading out a statement given to the family solicitor one year previously, she said the wedding of her daughter, Maureen, on 6 July 1985 had "passed off very well".

Fr Molloy, who she described as an "old family friend", attended the cold buffet lunch the day after the wedding, at around 3.30pm. He had also attended the wedding breakfast the previous day.

The priest had helped to clear off the tables after lunch. The bulk of lunch guests left sometime after 5pm and then she and her husband, Richard, and Fr Molloy visited their neighbours, the Goodbodys.

"We each had a small amount to drink there. We returned home from the Goodbodys about 9.30pm," she said.

Her daughter, Maureen, and daughter-in-law, Ann, left when the trio of friends returned to the house, while Auntie May was up but went to bed.

"We each had one or possibly two drinks in the sitting room at home. I was feeling very, very tired and said I wanted to go to bed.

It was suggested that we each have a night cap and Richard was to get these and bring them up to our bedroom. I went on upstairs on my own and changed into my nightclothes, took a sleeping pill and got into bed, I must have fallen asleep or dozed off," Therese said.

"I next remember Fr Molloy dressed in his sweater, shirt and trousers, sitting at the foot of the bed and Richard was sitting in bed beside me, dressed in his pyjamas. Richard and Fr Molloy were chatting. I do not now remember what the conversation was about and I cannot say if I joined in or how the conversation developed," she continued.

Her recollection of events, however, was hazy as she struggled to recall what happened on the night Niall died but remembered trying to revive her good friend.

"My next memory is of waking up or regaining consciousness on the floor of the bedroom. Fr Molloy was lying on the floor near the door. I was dazed and thought he must have passed out. I tried to lift him up and said he had better get to bed. He gave no sign of life. I tried to revive him. I listened for his heartbeat but heard none but I heard an awful gurgling sound. Richard was no longer in the room. I went out to the landing and called my husband," Mrs Flynn said.

"I do not remember what happened after that. I think I kept losing consciousness. I was hysterical and was brought to hospital and sedated," she added.

"When I was in hospital I became aware that I was badly bruised on my left arm and that I had an injury to my jaw. That is all I can remember."

Under cross-examination from the Molloy family's counsel, Therese said her recollection of events was no clearer since making her statement.

Niall's body was near the bedroom door when she first regained consciousness after being struck by her husband, she said.

"I know I lifted him by the shoulder. I lifted him up and I said I thought maybe he should get to bed. I thought at that stage he had passed out," Mrs Flynn said.

"I didn't see any sign of violence or blood. My brain was very addled and I was dazed," she further told the inquest.

She could not recall how long she had tried to resuscitate Fr Molloy. "I certainly tried my best and then I went on the landing. I could not understand why there was nobody else in the room. I went to the landing to call my husband," she said.

Mrs Flynn said she did not think of calling emergency services: "It didn't enter my head that there was anything like that wrong."

She further told Mr McKenna SC, representing the State, that she had little memory of what happened that night.

"I have no recollection from the time I went to bed. I remember distinctly enough going to bed and getting ready for bed. Then I must have gone to sleep. The next recollection I have is I woke up and saw Father sitting at the bottom of the bed and Richard beside me. Whether I dozed off or not I don't know," she told the inquest.

"My next recollection is myself lying on the floor and getting up," she continued.

Therese said she was the first to go to bed that night and she took a sleeping tablet and may have had another drink after that. "I could have taken a drink at that time. You see Richard was to bring me up a nightcap and I was sleeping when he brought it up, whether I took a sip when I woke up or not I can't say," she said.

Mrs Flynn said there was "nothing dramatic" about Fr Molloy's wounds when she awoke to find him on the floor.

She first learnt of Niall's death when her daughter Maureen told her several times that "Father is dead".

Mrs Flynn told the inquest that Niall had been kicked in the head when training a horse two years previously and was treated by Dr O'Sullivan.

Referring to the broken furniture found at Kilcoursey, she said the dining room table had been broken by a guest on the day of the wedding, while the coffee table had been broken by nephews when watching tennis that Sunday.

The final witness to take the stand was Richard Flynn.

In a statement to his solicitor, Richard said he had "nothing to add" to the interview notes taken by Inspector Monaghan on the night of Fr Molloy's death.

Reading his statement into the record, Mr Flynn outlined how a row had developed over drink.

"We all had quite an amount of drink taken. An argument developed between the three of us. It was a stupid argument over who would go downstairs for another drink. I refused to get them a drink but I said I was going to get one myself," he said.

He explained that he got out of bed to go downstairs when he was physically attacked by his wife and Niall and that he then struck back at them.

"My wife got out of bed and Fr Molloy, who was sitting in the room, got up to attack me. They both went for me at the same time and I struck both of them with my fists. I hit my wife once on the face and she fell down. I hit Fr Molloy at least twice and probably three times in the face with my clenched fists. Both my wife and Fr Molloy were rendered unconscious. I examined my wife and saw she was breathing. I also went to Fr Molloy and he was breathing with difficulty. I threw water on both their faces and said an act of contrition into Fr Molloy's ear. My wife revived but Fr Molloy did not. He was having difficulty and I knew he had a heart condition," he continued.

"I ran downstairs to phone the PP and Dr O'Sullivan. I got through to the PP, Fr Deignan, first. I could not get through to the doctor. I went back upstairs and my wife, Therese, said Fr Molloy was dead and she was in hysterics. I examined Fr Molloy and he was dead," the businessman said.

Richard said the parish priest, Fr Deignan, arrived almost immediately and Dr O'Sullivan, who was based in Kilbeggan, arrived shortly afterwards. Fr Deignan gave Fr Molloy the Last Rites and Mr Flynn asked the priest to notify the Gardaí.

Under cross-examination by the Molloy family's counsel, Mr Flynn said he had a clear recollection of events but that he could not remember who dragged Niall's body across the bedroom floor that night.

He confirmed that he had whispered the Act of Contrition into Fr Molloy's ear. "When I put my ear to his chest his pulse rate was very slow and I went then to call a doctor," he said, adding that he could not get through on the phone.

Asked why he did not call 999 or the emergency services, Richard said: "Because I had the doctor's numbers in my pocket."

Pressed on the matter when he could not get through to the doctor, he added: "It didn't occur to me."

Richard said he tried calling another local doctor, Dr Corboy.

He insisted it was the truth that his wife, Therese, and Fr Molloy attacked him at the same time, after he had refused to get them a drink.

He disputed having a conversation with Niall's brother, Billy, the day after his death in which he indicated that there had been a political row. "We did not discuss politics," Mr Flynn told the inquest.

The businessman said he struck Fr Molloy two or three times but no more than that. He was unclear as to whether the priest got up after being knocked down.

Asked about the medical evidence that suggested Fr Molloy was struck five to six blows, Richard said his friend may have fallen against a bedpost or TV table but he was unclear about what happened and did not elaborate on events.

Mr Flynn further denied a submission by Mr Charleton that he told Billy Molloy the following day that his brother, Niall, had fallen against the fireplace.

Some legal argument followed, in the absence of the jury, over the veracity of Billy Molloy's claim which had not been made in his statement to Gardaí. After some discussion, the coroner allowed questions about the fireplace and recalled the jury.

When re-examined about the matter, Richard again denied telling Billy that Niall hit his head against the fireplace after he had struck him.

He said he did not remember or see Fr Molloy falling but recalled defending himself against a punch from the priest. "I got one blow but I put up my hand to ward off the very first punch he threw at me and I got a mallet finger as a result," Mr Flynn told Mr Charleton, although he could not explain why Niall had no offensive marks.

"He may have fallen on to the newel post of the bed and when falling, bounced off the end of the bed, I don't know," he said.

Under sustained cross-examination, Richard said he struck his wife, Therese, first before striking the priest to the left jaw and then into the mouth. He did not notice any blood on Fr Molloy.

Asked if he was swinging wildly or aiming his punches, Mr Flynn said: "I was protecting myself. I was attacked by Fr Molloy viciously."

Because of "loss of memory", Richard could not remember what happened after he dealt the second blow to Niall. This memory lapse, he said, began after striking his friend in the mouth and his mind went completely blank.

Asked if anyone else could have struck the priest, Mr Flynn said nobody else was present.

His memory recovered, he said, when he saw Fr Molloy and his wife lying on the floor.

Under cross-examination by Mr McKenna, representing the State, Richard denied having a verbal row with Fr Molloy earlier that evening or ever telling Dr O'Sullivan there was a row downstairs.

Mr Flynn said he asked Fr Deignan to call the Gardaí after he had administered the Last Rites to Fr Molloy. "I knew I was delegating it to somebody in authority," he remarked.

The businessman said everything was amicable until an argument evolved over who would get the next drink. "My wife handed me her glass and asked me to get her a drink. I said I would. She said 'Won't you get a drink for Father?'. I said 'no' because he has a drink," Mr Flynn said.

He further told Mr McKenna: "I handed my wife back her own glass and said 'if you want a drink you'll get it yourself, I'll get mine. If Father wants a drink he can get his own'."

Up to that point everyone was in good humour, he said. "My wife was dozing. She didn't partake in the conversation in the bedroom, only Fr Molloy and myself," he said, adding that they were talking about going on holiday.

When Mr Flynn refused to get drinks for his wife and friend, Therese became abusive, he said.

"I turned for the door. I said I'd go to my own room," he told the inquest.

"They both charged at me. My wife turned on me. My wife got out of bed and both of them, Fr Molloy got up from where he was sitting, and they both charged at me," he added.

He said he was "very surprised" by what happened. On realising that both were unconscious on the floor, he threw water on their faces.

Richard offered little by way of explanation for the blood stains evident around the room.

"The only way I can account for it is it must be as a result of me getting the water in the bathroom, after that there must have been blood on my hands," he said.

Under further cross-examination by his own counsel, Mr Connolly, Mr Flynn said he was barefoot on the night and, to his knowledge, he did not kick Fr Molloy.

The 48-year-old said he enlisted the services of a psychiatrist, Dr Hanniffy, in a bid to help him to remember what happened on the night.

On his conversation with Billy the day after Niall died, he again denied saying there was a political row. "I told him we were friends for years and I was very sorry for what happened. It was a terrible accident," he said.

The coroner then re-examined Mr Flynn about what may have sparked off the "sudden explosion" between the three friends who were happily discussing their next holiday to Normandy and if there was anything else simmering under the surface.

Richard said there was not, but suggested his wife's exhaustion may have been a factor. "I think it was the over-tiredness of my wife. She was exhausted," he said, adding that she had taken a sleeping pill downstairs before going to bed.

DAY THREE: SATURDAY, 26 JULY 1986.

As the inquest entered its third day, it was drawing to a close. While a number of witnesses were not called, all evidence had been heard.

Closing legal submissions were made before the jury of nine men and three women were charged to deliberate on what they heard.

Summing up, the Deputy Coroner Mr Mahon said the evidence suggested that Fr Molloy had died at around 1am on 8 July and that the "stopped watch theory" amounted to "very dangerous" conjecture that was not supported by evidence from Gardaí attending the post-mortem.

Before charging the jury with the task of deliberating on the evidence, the coroner highlighted the consistent and inconsistent facts of the case, while also sharing his own thoughts on events.

Mr Mahon said he understood why a priest was the first person alerted to Fr Molloy's death and why Fr Deignan spoke of a scandal in the parish to Sergeant Forde but asserted that what transpired did not amount to a "cover-up".

"It was a manifestation of Fr Deignan's alarm at what had happened and his concern for a fellow priest, being found in that position, as say a doctor might feel for another doctor or a lawyer might feel for another lawyer, but even more so for a priest being so found because of his position in the community," Mr Mahon commented.

The coroner went on to say he understood why the Flynns sought Dr O'Sullivan rather than looking for another doctor or seeking an ambulance. And while he understood the delay in contacting the police, he stressed that he could not condone it.

Highlighting the inconsistencies in the case, the coroner noted the eight-foot-long bloody drag mark on the bedroom carpet, which remained unexplained, as did the intense and furious row that erupted between the three friends.

"I can only believe that something gave rise to that eruption of anger by one, two or all of those present and this inquiry has not been told what that was," Mr Mahon said.

On the medical evidence, Mr Mahon offered two possible verdicts, which were not mutually exclusive. Niall may have died from acute brain swelling and subdural haemorrhage consistent with a sustained serious injury to the head or an abnormally enlarged heart muscle may have contributed to his death.

The inquest jury retired at 11.55am that Saturday morning to consider the evidence. Within 13 minutes they returned with a unanimous verdict that Fr Molloy died from head injuries and not from heart issues.

The verdict was greeted with applause by Fr Molloy's family, friends and parishioners in the courtroom. Richard and Therese Flynn were not present but their son, David, extended the family's sympathy on Fr Molloy's death.

Outside the courtroom, the late priest's nephew, Ian Maher, told waiting media that the family were satisfied with the outcome but that questions remained.

Commenting on the "bizarre" memory lapses suffered by the Flynns in the witness box, Mr Maher told the *Sunday Independent*: "I think the public will draw their own conclusions from Mr and Mrs Flynn's evidence."

###

Several other witnesses gave statements to the inquest but were not called to give evidence, including David, Zandra and Anita Flynn and James Lowry, the groom at Kilcoursey House.

Relatives of Fr Molloy, his brother, Billy, and niece, Suzannah Allen, who gave depositions, were also not called to give evidence.

Other statements not included were from staff at Tullamore Hospital where Therese Flynn was admitted and treated on the night.

In a memo of an interview with Gardaí, Dr Frank Durkan, a consultant surgeon at Tullamore General Hospital, said Mrs Flynn was admitted in the early hours of 8 July after receiving "a box in the face".

Dr Durkan told Gardaí he could provide a medical report with Therese's consent but subsequently confirmed that he was instructed by Mrs Flynn's solicitor not to do so.

In his medical report Dr Liam Hanniffy, Chief Psychiatrist, St. Fintan's Hospital, Portlaoise, said Therese was admitted at around 4am and that he examined her following referral by Dr Durkan.

"She had the appearance of a semi-conscious condition and she was on an intravenous drip. She was unable to speak or keep her eyes open. She tried a number of times to speak to me but she could not verbalise. However, she appeared to understand me and when I referred to the death of her friend she shed tears," Dr Hanniffy's report stated.

He said Mrs Flynn's condition improved the following day but she had no recollection of being examined the previous day and she could not recall events immediately prior to admission.

In the doctor's case records, he noted "amnesia" persisting on 11 July but that Therese did not require hospitalisation and could be discharged home.

Dr Hanniffy concluded that she was suffering from an "hysterical dissociative reaction" with amnesia as a marked feature.

His notes also cited an authority on this diagnosis, an American psychiatrist Laurence C Kolb, who said associative amnesia was not merely forgetting: "It is an active process, a blotting out of awareness of unpleasant features. Periods of stupor or of twilight state may precede such an amnesia, which tends to become selective and limited to the particular element or experience that evoked it."

Other evidence not furnished at the trial or inquest included laboratory analysis of Therese's blood on the night of her admission to Tullamore hospital. Blood test results revealed an alcohol level of 220mg of alcohol per 100mls of blood – over twice the legal limit for driving at the time and higher than Fr Molloy's. Also, laboratory tests did not detect any barbiturates or sedatives in her blood, despite Therese claiming to have taken a sleeping pill before bed and being purportedly sedated by Dr O'Sullivan that night.

While the inquest verdict was a hard-won victory for the Molloy family, it compounded the fact that the truth of what happened that night remained unknown and justice had not been served.

In addition to the hazy recollection of events by Richard and Therese Flynn, fresh evidence of a row downstairs, broken furniture, and the possibility that Fr Molloy fell against the fireplace raised even more questions.

Niall's brother, Billy, remained so disillusioned by the criminal justice system that in the wake of the diverging trial and inquest outcomes he was making plans to emigrate and become a US citizen.

Billy told the *Cork Examiner* that the inquest verdict had "vindicated the family's efforts to find the truth" but that the trial result had left a "very bitter aftertaste". The family, he said, intended to take a civil suit against Mr Flynn.

"It was all worth it when I heard the verdict and the relief we feel is unbelievable. What we knew all the time is now official," Billy remarked.

Flanked by his wife and family, Billy added: "From what we could gauge from the public's reaction, the people of this country were genuinely concerned and frightened by the case as they felt there was a miscarriage of justice."

While the Molloy family planned to take a break, they gave the green light for a legal team to start working on a civil suit, as Billy explained: "Behind the scenes our legal team will be working at the possibility of taking civil action against the Flynns not only for Fr Niall's property, including sports trophies and other sentimental items which we believe are still in his rooms at Kilcoursey House, but also for the loss of a good brother and the distress caused by that loss."

Looking back today, Molloy family solicitor Ben O'Raftery said the inquest verdict brought some relief but also raised even more questions: "It meant I suppose that the criminal trial should have been let run to a full conclusion. That's putting it at its simplest, that's what it meant to the family," he told the recent documentary about Niall's death.

The only comment from the Flynn family about Fr Molloy's death was made by David to RTÉ correspondent Tom McCaughren after the inquest concluded. He sympathised with the Molloys and the parishioners of Castlecoote on Niall's death, and then said, "It's very difficult, maybe, when one knows certain answers and isn't in a position to comment. It makes it very difficult to live with."

Chapter 4
FRIENDS IN HIGH PLACES

The Telephone Café in Brooklyn was packed with supporters and willing donors to the campaign for Irish freedom. Influential contacts and favours were called in all over New York to ensure Eamon de Valera, who would later become President of an independent and free Irish Republic, received a large and lucrative reception. This was circa 1919 and William Molloy, an emigrant from the west of Ireland who was now a successful businessman, was happy to play his part in de Valera's US fundraising tour. William had himself grafted for the cause and was also a friend of John Devoy, a prominent Irish Republican and rebel. De Valera never showed up on the day, however, instead choosing to stay in Boston. Outraged, embarrassed and disillusioned, William vowed never to help 'Dev' again.

Niall's father, William J Molloy was born near Claremorris in Mayo in 1884, the second of 13 children, and the eldest boy. By the age of 17, he was working in his uncle's shop in Tuam, Co Galway. In March 1905, he married Agnes Lavan and in November, their daughter Maureen was born. Tragically, Agnes passed away six months later, as a result of complications from the delivery. Distraught and ready for a new life, William left baby Maureen with Agnes' parents and travelled on the Oceanic liner from Cobh to New York, arriving to stay with his Uncle Martin in Brooklyn in September 1906.

His brother, James, joined him in 1908 and that same year, William applied for US citizenship. In 1912, he married Susanna Maneely, who had also emigrated to the US from Mayo. They both became American citizens in 1913.

In 1915, William became the owner of The Telephone Café at the corner of Fulton Street and Rockaway Avenue in Brooklyn. Also known as 'The Molloy Brothers' Café', it proved popular as a bar for locals and the Irish-American community. By 1920, William and Susanna had bought their own home in Brooklyn and had four children, Eileen, Sue, James (Brod) and Veronica.

The success of the bar was threatened, however, when Prohibition – a blanket ban on the production, importation, transportation and sale of alcohol – was introduced across the United States. The Telephone Café had to become a less profitable dry goods store and in light of this, and the potential for independence back home, James, then William and Susanna, decided to move back to Ireland.

On returning, they put down new roots in Co Roscommon. William bought Carrowroe House on the outskirts of Roscommon town, a large country residence previously owned by Major Thomas Goff, an Anglo-Irish landlord, farmer and politician. Goff had served as the High Sheriff of Roscommon and a Deputy Lieutenant for County Roscommon but was selling up to return to England as the Irish War of Independence was coming to a close.

At Carrowroe, William farmed the land and he and James set up a hardware store and a bakery on Main Street in Roscommon in 1922. The Molloy brothers became big employers and were well-regarded in the community.

In addition to building the business, William pursued his interest in politics, honed when he was involved in the 'Friends of Ireland in America' campaign. In 1922, he became a Senator in the first Irish Senate and served as an independent until 1931, alongside high-profile Irish figures, such as WB Yeats, Henry Guinness, Oliver St. John Gogarty, and Douglas Hyde, who would become the first President of Ireland.

Meanwhile, his business interests continued to grow and he invested in stocks and shares, as well as a cinema in the nearby town of Castlerea. He still had property in the US and he would occasionally visit his eldest daughter Maureen, who had emigrated and married in Long Island.

William and Susanna had four more children while living in Roscommon – Billy, Alice, Pauline and Niall, the youngest.

While they were expected to know the value of hard work by helping on the farm, the three boys and five girls enjoyed a comfortable background and upbringing.

Niall shared his parents' love of horses and developed an interest in show jumping, winning the Claremorris Show when he was just 14 years old. He was adored by his sisters and mother. As a child they dressed him up and played with him and when sent to work in the fields as he grew older, he invariably ended up back at the house in the company of his sisters – his excuse was that he was going back to organise lunch for the workers. Nobody really seemed to mind.

###

Meanwhile, in Galway, the Brennan family were carving out a name in the drapery sector.

In 1907 a young Martin Brennan moved from Ennis to Galway to work for his uncle, who owned a shop in the city. Martin built up the business, establishing Martin Brennan & Co. with drapery shops in Galway city and Salthill. He married Bridget and they went on to have six children, five girls and one boy. Initially they lived in Prospect Hill in Galway but later moved to Belmont House in Renmore. The Brennan daughters – Therese, Ita, Cecily, Angela and Frances – were well known in social and show jumping circles. Therese Brennan was an accomplished horsewoman from an early age, and along with her sisters, took part in hunts, gymkhanas and shows.

On the other side of Galway, in Turloughmore, near Lackagh, Thomas Kearney founded a business encompassing a shop, pub, hardware and animal feed store in 1842. Passing it on from generation to generation, his granddaughter, Maureen Kearney, eventually took it over from her father, Richard, in the 1930s. The business grew in size, reach and reputation, and was a big employer in the area. When Maureen married Thomas Flynn, a farmer from Tubber in Offaly, the business changed its name from Kearney's to Flynns of Lackagh. In the 1950s their son, Michael, took over the store and expanded it further, while their other son Richard made his name playing rugby for Connaught and taking part in the odd equestrian event.

These histories provide a glimpse of the comfortable upbringing that Niall, Therese and Richard enjoyed as the children of successful business owners.

Socialising in the same circles, the trio first met as teenagers on the pony club circuit. By then, Niall was attending Summerhill College in Sligo – a Diocesan College and feeder school for the priesthood. Past pupils include former Taoiseach and Fianna Fáil TD Albert Reynolds, Edward J. Flanagan, who founded the Boys Town orphanages in the US, tenor John McCormack and members of the pop band Westlife.

Niall's future seemed to have been mapped out for him. His eldest brother, James, or Brod as he was known, was to inherit Carrowroe, Billy started a haulage and car hire business, and his sisters married and settled down. At the time, it was common to have a member of the clergy – a priest or nun – in the family. With Niall's gentle nature and lack of interest in pursuing a specific career that was not equestrian in nature, he became the obvious candidate. It was his mother's wish and, for Niall, he was happy to go along with it.

While Niall took up his religious studies in Maynooth, and then Rome, Therese attended university where she studied agriculture. It was there that she became close friends with Anne Devine, who would later marry Brian Lenihan, the prominent Fianna Fáil politician.

In the intervening years, Richard and Therese married in 1955, with their Salthill wedding featuring in social columns in both national and local newspapers.

One report described Therese's dress in detail: "The bride wore a pearl embroidered Chantilly lace gown, carried out on Elizabethan lines, with formal train. Her tulle, waist-length veil was surmounted by a diamante and pearl headdress. Bridesmaids wore American nylon tulle frocks in white, lemon and pink, showered with pink rosebuds, carried out with draped shoulder line, tight fitting ruched bodice and very full skirts, with which they wore matching tulle headdresses." The couple honeymooned in Switzerland.

Niall was ordained in Rome in 1957. He was one of 19 students in the Irish College there and the whole Molloy family travelled over for the auspicious occasion. The ordination was even broadcast on Radio Eireann, as it was then, with a follow-up request programme.

On Niall's return, he and a fellow Roscommon cleric, Fr James Casey, were welcomed with bonfires lit along the road leading into the town and further celebrations.

From similar middle-class backgrounds, Richard, Therese and Niall had a lot in common. Their families were of a certain standing in Irish society and were considered well-heeled and well-connected.

When Therese's sister, Ita, married Noel Griffin of Waterford Glass in 1959 it featured prominently in the press. His father, Joseph Griffin, was in the IRA's Dublin Brigade during the War of Independence and fought against the Anglo–Irish Treaty. After running his own accounting practice, he became Controller of Prices for the Fianna Fáil-led government during the Emergency of 1939-1945. The guest list at Noel and Ita's wedding included Taoiseach Sean Lemass, Tánaiste Seán McEntee and Minister for Agriculture Patrick Smith. Noel and Ita bought Mount Kennedy House in Wicklow, where they lived until Noel's sudden death in 1981.

The connections were not only political, though. There were several members of the clergy within the Molloy, Brennan and

Flynn families. One person, although not a family member, was a constant in the life of Fr Molloy – Roscommon native Bishop Dominic Conway, who had taught Niall and was a regular visitor to Carrowroe House over the years.

Studying in the Irish College in Rome was a privilege held for priests who showed promise and a capacity for deep theological learning, and for those who could afford it. While Niall was neither a bookworm or noted scholar, his father's wealth ensured he would receive the best opportunities. Priests who studied and were ordained in Rome were, at the time, destined for special posts, although Fr Molloy's comfortable background was a source of unease for some, including Bishop Conway.

As a newly ordained priest, Niall took up his first post in the parish of Loughrea before being moved to Athlone, then Highwood near Boyle, and then to Tibohine in the early 1960s.

When Senator William Molloy died in 1965 he left a substantial fortune, some of which had already been passed onto Niall before his death.

Some family members believed that Niall was left as much as IR£65,000 – a sizeable sum at the time and worth in the region of €1.6million today. It may have been in the form of shares in Cement Roadstone Holdings. Even if it had only been one-tenth of that, it would have been more than enough to give Niall the means to pursue his interest in horses. In the years that followed, Niall used the money to invest in property, land, paintings and antiques. While it was unusual for a priest to have business interests, diocesan orders were not obliged to take a vow of poverty, so Niall was not in breach of any Church rules. For Niall, it was about his love of horses rather than turning a profit or living the high life.

In September 1970, Niall took the opportunity to serve as Army Chaplain in Custume Barracks in Athlone. The post would offer him a very different set of responsibilities than those of a diocesan priest. While he was Chaplain, Niall was chief celebrant of the 55th anniversary of the 1916 Rising in Arbour Hill, where President Eamon de Valera – the man who stood his father up in New York over 50 years earlier – was the guest of honour. Also in attendance was Brian Lenihan Senior and other high-profile members of Fianna Fáil, who were in government at the time.

During his time as army chaplain, Niall served seven months in Cyprus as part of a United Nations peacekeeping mission with the 23rd Infantry Group in October 1972. Before leaving for Cyprus, Niall needed to find somewhere to keep his two horses while he was away and he turned to his friends Richard and Therese Flynn, who lived relatively close to Athlone. At the time, the Flynns lived at Tober House, where they had acres of land, stables and the facilities to look after the horses and it was around this time that the business relationship between Niall and Therese was forged.

Niall was happy in the Army. He felt more comfortable dealing directly with the spiritual needs of soldiers than in a parish environment, where his shyness made it difficult for him to be the public face of the Church, calling to parishioners' homes or visiting the ill in hospital. In April 1975, however, he was moved from his post in the Army by the Bishop of Elphin Dominic Conway – a decision that caused him a great deal of stress. The decision meant he could not qualify for an Army pension. In return for his untimely removal from the army post, Niall's request for a move to the parish of Fuerty was granted. He would be based in the village of Castlecoote, near his sister, Pauline, and a short distance from Roscommon town and his relatives.

Niall settled back into parish responsibilities, whilst also pursuing his interest in horses. When he first arrived in Fuerty, the parochial house was virtually falling down. The floor of his bedroom collapsed, forcing him to live in a caravan while the parish came together to fundraise to build a new bungalow beside the church.

"He was very active in a practical way; he started a pony club for the children and paid for a church organ for the choir. While he was very happy to fulfil his parish duties and go over and above them at times, he wasn't comfortable dropping in and out of people's houses. He had a handful of close friends, but never overstayed his welcome," Niall O'Connor, a nephew of the late priest explained.

While Fr Molloy was reared with a "silver spoon", his friend and local parishioner, Mamie Delaney, has fond memories of the gentle curate: "He was so easy, and gentle, gentle is a big thing in his life. And he was somebody you could trust and you felt very much at home with him. It didn't matter if he walked in here and the spuds were on the table. He wasn't one of those who looked for perfection, he accepted everything.

"Everybody respected him and looked up to him but he didn't demand anything special from anybody, you know he was that kind of person who'd fit in with any kind of situation," she added.

Niall was a benevolent force within the parish and many children still recall his easy manner and gentleness when they made their First Communion with him. Local children also loved sharing the news of Santa's gifts after Christmas Mass and he never rushed them as they told their magical stories.

He became embedded in the life of the village. Every Monday morning, the priest would meet with Fianna Fáil politician Terry Leyden, and the owner of Castlecoote Stores, Mark Delaney, for a weekly discussion about the affairs of the parish. They got things done. At this level, Niall was organised, focused and determined, ensuring everything and everyone was looked after properly.

It was Fr Molloy's generosity and gentle nature that made him a hit with local parishioners, as his friend Nonie Golden recalls: "Had he been less generous with his parishioners, or less gentle, he may not have been forgiven his 'landed gentry' other life. That was his upbringing, and while he could live frugally, his love of horses and talent with them meant he was moving in a different social circle completely."

This was old money, mixed with the new Irish middle class who emerged from Ireland's independence of the 1920s. People like his father, who had done well in business, aligned themselves politically, and their success was evident through their stately homes and country estates.

Niall's love for horses, and his achievements with them, were well-known in Castlecoote. It was also not unusual for his friends, Therese and Richard, to visit, and Therese frequently bought feed and supplies from Castlecoote Stores.

In many respects, Fr Molloy's lifestyle was carefree. Once he had taken care of parish duties, he was free to focus on his passion for horses. He was free to drive to the Flynn homestead, Kilcoursey House in Clara, where he could come and go as he pleased.

Niall had served as President of Roscommon Equestrian Club, Chairman of County Roscommon Hunt, a committee member of South Westmeath Hunt, a committee member of Connacht region Show Jumping Association of Ireland, a member of the regional training committee, Connacht Disciplinary Committee, and as a National Pony selector and regional representative on the National Pony Committee.

In the year before his death, Niall managed the Irish Pony Team at the European Championships and was Chef D'equipe of the Connacht team and the RDS Spring Show. He was also awarded a Roscommon Sports Award for his equestrian endeavours and was named 'Roscommon Man of the Year' just months before he was killed in 1985.

Chapter 5
THE MISSING FILES

In the wake of the dramatic trial and inquest in 1986, the Molloy case took another peculiar twist – one that allegedly involved notorious crime boss Martin Cahill, otherwise known as 'The General'.

In late August 1987, the Molloy case once again hit the headlines when the Office of the Director of Public Prosecutions (DPP), on St Stephen's Green in the heart of Dublin, was ransacked and dozens of files were stolen.

The bizarre break-in occurred over the weekend – between 5.30pm on Friday 29 August and 9.05am on Sunday 31 August – when security detail was non-existent.

Astonishingly, it emerged at the time that while Gardaí routinely patrolled the building during the day, the DPP's Office had been left without any security detail at night for the previous two years.

In addition to questions over how potentially sensitive files were stored and secured, the break-in also sparked fears that details of Garda informants may have been stolen.

An exhaustive investigation was mounted by Gardaí from Harcourt Street, along with staff from the DPP's Office, to establish what files were missing.

Initial reports suggested that more than 100 files were stolen and it quickly transpired that the Molloy file was among them, along with documents relating to other high-profile cases, such as the double-murderer Malcolm MacArthur.

When questions were asked about the theft of sensitive information in the Molloy case, a spokesperson for the Office of the DPP suggested the family seek reassurance in writing from the Office, but insisted that the DPP could not comment publicly on the break-in.

Not only was it embarrassing for the minority Fianna Fáil government of the day, but it provided political fodder for TDs from the opposing benches.

Justice spokesperson for the Progressive Democrats, Deputy Mary Harney, said the burglary raised serious questions: "While the theft of so many files may have occurred in order to hide the identity of those involved it may also be the case that this was done by a criminal organisation whose purpose was to undermine our present judicial system."

Fine Gael justice spokesman Tom Enright also questioned why the most senior law office of the State was left unprotected: "Undoubtedly, confidential information contained in the 100 stolen files will be of benefit to criminal and subversive organisations."

His Fine Gael colleague, Alan Shatter, who was spokesman on law reform, joined in the chorus of politicians seeking greater clarity on the DPP burglary as well as another recent faux pas in which a Garda memo of the British Ambassador's holiday arrangements had been leaked.

"An urgent statement should now be made by the government answering the many questions raised by these grave, unbelievable, bizarre and unprecedented events," Deputy Shatter said.

It was subsequently confirmed that close to 150 files had been taken in the brazen burglary for which nobody was charged.

Months later, the then Justice Minister Gerry Collins gave little away when pressed for an update in the Dáil. "In this case I will confine my remarks to saying that the Garda authorities have indicated that practically all files in the Office appeared to have been disturbed and that 145 files were stolen," Minister Collins said.

"These include some files dealing with particular cases of note submitted by the Garda to the Director of Public Prosecutions and some of a more general nature," he added.

The Justice Minister, however, maintained that the issue of security was not a matter for his department: "As regards the question of security arrangements, the position is that the security of the premises in question is primarily a matter for the owners or occupiers of the premises and not the responsibility of the Minister for Justice. I do not, in any event, believe that it would be in the public interest to give details of the security arrangements in place in any particular instance."

The lapse in security at the DPP offices in 1987 was not the first breach to come to public attention.

In April 1986 the DPP came under fire for a security blunder in which a dossier on the private lives of prison officers at the high-security prison in Portlaoise was mistakenly handed to IRA prisoners, according to press reports.

The security gaffes occurred at a time when concerns were raised internally about "staff requirements" in the DPP's Office, how it was funded, and the need for restructuring. The Office was still relatively new, having only been established in 1975.

While the DPP, Eamon Barnes, dismissed allegations that his Office was at fault for the "major blunder", he acknowledged it did require more resources and facilities.

###

More than five years later, some but not all of the stolen DPP files were recovered.

All along, Gardaí believed that The General had masterminded the 1987 burglary, although they never secured sufficient evidence to charge him for it.

The Dubliner had come to the attention of Gardaí over many years, not least for his role in targeting the chief forensic scientist Dr James O'Donovan with a car bomb in 1982.

Martin Cahill's infamous exploits included high-profile heists, such as the IR£2 million theft from O'Connor's Jewellers in 1983 and later, in 1986, the daring robbery of eighteen priceless paintings from the Beit collection at Russborough House in County Wicklow, which included Dutch Masters, such as Vermeer and Rubens, among others.

In 1988, The General came to national prominence and became a household name when the *Today Tonight* current affairs programme on RTE interviewed the criminal kingpin, who was under 24-hour surveillance by Gardaí.

That same year, he landed himself with a four-month stint in Spike Island prison for breaching the peace after he verbally abused neighbours during the ongoing round-the-clock Garda surveillance.

In a curious twist, Judge Frank Roe, who presided over the trial of Richard Flynn, came face to face with The General himself and the criminal's brother in the late 1980s.

In February 1988, just months after the burglary of the DPP's Office, Judge Roe dealt with The General's brother, Michael Cahill, a father-of-two and heroin addict, who pleaded guilty to receiving more than IR£13,000 in cash and foreign currency, the proceeds of crime.

Bank officials at a Dublin airport branch grew suspicious when he and another man tried to change cash into a number of different currencies and alerted Gardaí, who discovered that the cash was linked to a robbery at a Grafton Street bank three years earlier.

Pleading for leniency, Cahill's defence counsel, Patrick McEntee SC, told the court his client was dependent on heroin and that the "mindless" crime reflected his desperation for cash.

Handing down a five-year prison sentence, Judge Roe said: "I do not think that any significant reduction in sentence should be given if a man commits a violent crime or helps others in the commission of one just because he is a heroin addict. Cahill has a bad record."

A year later, Judge Roe dealt directly with The General himself, who appeared before the circuit court to appeal a fine of IR£75 for a parking offence.

During the appeal hearing, Cahill denied being abusive to Gardaí, who approached him about his car causing a traffic obstruction. "I didn't swear at anyone. But I admit having my hand to my face, which I always do," Cahill told the court.

"I was told I was obstructing traffic but I am always sure never to do anything wrong in my car because the Gardaí are always behind me," he added.

On hearing the facts, Judge Roe said he had no doubt that Cahill had caused an obstruction, and upheld the fine but reluctantly, yet remarkably, lifted an endorsement on The General's driving licence because it was a first offence under the Road Traffic Act.

###

The stolen DPP documents didn't resurface until the early 1990s when some of the 145 missing files were recovered following confidential tip-offs to police.

In 1994 the stolen Molloy file began to make headlines again. The General was assassinated in his car in August that year and, in the wake of his death, *Sunday Independent* journalist Veronica Guerin made some startling revelations about the file and what it contained.

Guerin, who had been exposing the underbelly of Dublin's criminal world, claimed that she saw a 'top secret' Garda file on the Molloy case, among the stash allegedly stolen by Cahill.

In a series of extraordinary articles, Guerin shed fresh light on aspects of the Molloy case and made astonishing claims that Cahill had done a deal with authorities to return the Molloy file in exchange for the release of John Traynor, his close criminal associate, from a high-security prison in England in the early 1990s.

The fearless investigative journalist, who was murdered two years later, claimed to have seen photocopies of documents from the Molloy file, which The General had allegedly kept as bargaining material.

Years later, Cahill's daughter, Frances, lent some weight to Guerin's claims in her 2007 book, *Martin Cahill, My Father.*

In the book, Frances recalled how her father had taken a great interest in the Molloy case and had discussed it with Guerin before his death.

"My father recalled that the priest's head had been bashed in with the statue of a horse, information that allegedly came from the DPP's file on the case," she wrote.

Ms Cahill also spoke to Gardaí when they mounted a fresh probe into Niall's death in 2010 and recalled the time her father discussed the Molloy file with her.

Two decades later, a subsequent review of the case considered the 1994 assertions made by Veronica Guerin about the stolen Molloy file.

Senior Counsel Dominic McGinn, who reviewed the findings of a more recent Garda inquiry into Niall's death, verified that The General and his gang were implicated in the 1987 theft of the DPP files.

In his 2015 report, Mr McGinn confirmed that Cahill and other known criminal suspects were arrested in relation to the stolen DPP files but that no charges were brought due to insufficient evidence.

It was an "undeniable fact", he said, that the Molloy file was stolen but that there was no evidence to suggest that the file was targeted in the burglary.

His report suggested that the stolen Molloy file was recovered in January 1993, among 60 files retrieved from a premises on Arbour Hill on Dublin's northside following a confidential tip-off to Gardaí.

The Molloy family, however, maintain that the stolen DPP file was returned separately and was collected by Gardaí by arrangement. It was allegedly left in a hedge near the Garda Club on Harrington Street in Dublin city centre. "The Molloy file was not recovered as part of a batch of files but was left in a hedge for collection by Gardaí, apparently in a Dunnes Stores bag," Niall's nephew Bill Maher recalled.

The claims of The General using the file to barter with authorities is also covered in several books down through the years.

###

The year of the break-in at the DPP's Office was another difficult period for the Molloy family, who lost Billy, Niall's brother, at just 62 years of age.

Billy Molloy, who was consumed with getting to the truth of what happened in Kilcoursey House, died 10 days after being diagnosed with a perforated colon.

He passed away in May 1987, less than two years after his younger brother's life had come to a violent and brutal end.

Billy's children today recall how their father was left "broken" by what happened to Niall and the many questions that remained unanswered.

His son, Fr Billy Molloy, who became a priest after Niall's untimely death, described his father as a "shell of a man" after the trial and inquest.

"It was heart-breaking to see my father broken. He was always very strong willed and determined. That was gone. He became obsessed, a manic obsession about what's going on and what didn't go on and what happened and who told lies and who did this and who did that," Billy said.

Liz Molloy said her father never came to terms with Niall's death and the events that followed. "He never got over it. Once he got the news the first day he was determined to try and solve it himself because nothing was working fast enough for him," Liz recalled.

In the end, the search for answers took its toll on his business and health.

"He had a good business, the haulage business, but he just had to sell it in the end because he'd lost interest in it. He just wasn't able for it, this had taken over his life completely, the quest for answers that were never answered," she added.

While the Molloy family grieved the loss of Billy so soon after Niall, they also considered legal action against the Flynns and tried, in vain, to establish the full extent of Fr Molloy's assets and business dealings.

In August 1987, the family launched a civil suit against Richard Flynn for expenses and special damages relating to Niall's death.

With Billy gone, Ian Maher, took up the mantle to press for answers about his uncle's death. He was also the administrator of the late priest's estate.

Within months, the case was in the headlines again.

In April 1988, the civil action against Richard Flynn was heard before Tullamore Circuit Court and the Molloy family was awarded a settlement of IR£13,141.

Around the same time, there were fresh revelations that Therese Flynn had allegedly tried to cash in on a life insurance policy in Niall's name, which named her as his sister.

In the wake of the civil case, the Molloy family initiated further High Court proceedings for the return of the IR£12,000 deposit paid by Niall in the 1984 land deal. "Trying to sort out Niall's affairs is like trying to go through an obstacle course but we are determined to see this through to the end," Mr Maher commented at the time.

More crucially, the Molloy family pushed for the case to be reopened and presented Gardaí with new medical evidence that Niall may have survived for several hours before dying from the injuries he had sustained.

A pathologist had independently reviewed the autopsy files and samples of Fr Molloy's brain tissue to find that the priest may have been kicked as well as punched prior to his death.

The Molloy family went public with this significant new information in a bid to crack the case wide open again.

Their renewed pleas for a fresh investigation into Niall's death, however, proved futile as there was little appetite to resurrect the high-profile case.

Responding to calls in the Dáil for the case to be reopened, the Justice Minister Gerry Collins played down any new developments or evidence in the case: "I am informed by the Garda Commissioner that the position is still as indicated in the statement issued on his behalf on 26 April 1988 — no official complaint or additional evidence has been received by the Gardaí in this matter. Should such a complaint be made, or should additional evidence be forthcoming, it will be considered."

Despite the Molloy family's best efforts, interest in the case faded for several years until 1994 when fresh revelations emerged about the stolen DPP file and the judge at the centre of Richard Flynn's shock acquittal, Judge Thomas Frank Roe.

Chapter 6
A CONFLICT OF INTEREST

In 1986, Judge Frank Roe's controversial ruling at Richard Flynn's trial brought pressure on the government and the legal offices of the State to offer some explanation for the diverging outcomes of the trial and inquest.

The inquest verdict into Fr Niall Molloy's death had turned the trial result, just weeks earlier, on its head and led to calls in the Dáil for greater transparency and accountability across the criminal justice system.

The Molloy case also brought some of Judge Roe's more recent rulings into sharper focus.

As the hard-won inquest verdict dominated the newspaper headlines another case involving Judge Roe also attracted attention.

The front page of the *Evening Herald* on Saturday, 26 July 1986 led with the Fr Molloy inquest verdict as well as the fallout from a hit-and-run court case also involving Judge Roe.

The judge allowed a disqualified driver, who knocked down and killed a five-year-old boy in Dublin, to walk free from court, causing public outcry.

The parents of Philip Bailey, from Tallaght in Dublin, were

distraught over what they described as a "disgraceful" ruling by the judge, who had handed down a 25-year driving ban but allowed the already disqualified driver to walk free.

"It's hard to understand how a man who drove over a child and then tried to run away could get off like this," Gerard Bailey remarked at the time.

The Roe rulings in the Molloy and Bailey cases fuelled concerns in political circles, with the Justice spokesperson for the Progressive Democrats, Mary Harney, raising both with the Oireachtas Committee on Crime and Lawlessness.

Deputy Harney raised a motion on the need for members of the judiciary and the Director of Public Prosecutions to explain their decisions.

Public confidence in the judicial process, she said, had been "seriously undermined" in recent times and there was "no opportunity for proper public debate on a large number of serious issues relating to justice and law enforcement".

While the independence of judges could not be interfered with, she said "judges owe a corresponding duty to make their decisions clear and comprehensible".

If necessary, legislation should be introduced to ensure that juries can deliberate on all questions of fact in such cases, she said, adding that the verdict in the Tullamore inquest into Fr Molloy's death had fully vindicated the public's confidence in the jury system.

"The role both of judges and of those who give expert evidence, medical or otherwise, should be to assist and guide the jury but not to substitute their view," Deputy Harney said.

The calls for greater accountability and transparency, however, failed to precipitate legislative change at that time.

###

Eight years later, Judge Roe returned to the media spotlight when fresh claims of an alleged conflict of interest in the Molloy case emerged.

As detailed earlier, in 1994 *Sunday Independent* journalist Veronica Guerin made some startling claims about the Garda file on the case that was stolen from the DPP's Office in 1987.

In addition to claims that Martin Cahill, aka The General, used the file to bargain with authorities, Guerin also claimed that Judge Roe was allegedly compromised in the Molloy case and should have recused himself from hearing it.

Judge Roe, she said, wrote to DPP Eamon Barnes before the trial advising that he was known to the Flynns and Fr Molloy.

The claim was based on a handwritten letter from Judge Roe, contained in the stolen Garda file, which was dated before charges were brought against Richard Flynn.

Guerin further claimed that the Molloy file also included a second letter from Judge Roe, which explained his ruling and direction to acquit Mr Flynn of all charges in connection to Fr Molloy's death.

When Judge Roe was contacted by Guerin for comment at the time, he had nothing to say except that the case was "dead and buried". Asked about the letters, Judge Roe's only comment to Guerin was that Fr Molloy and the Flynns were "lovely people" and "God bless them all".

Two years after the claims about Judge Roe emerged, Guerin was shot dead in broad daylight as she was stopped at a traffic light in Dublin. She was murdered by the very criminals she had been exposing through her work.

While nothing came of the conflict of interest allegations in the 1990s, they were subsequently considered as part of a government-commissioned review of the Molloy case in more recent years.

In 2015, Senior Counsel Dominic McGinn, who reviewed available evidence and new information gathered by Gardaí, looked at the claims, as well as how Judge Roe dealt with the Flynn trial in 1986.

In his review, he found that Judge Roe's ruling – to direct the jury to acquit Richard Flynn on all charges – was an "extraordinary" intervention but was also within the law.

Judge Roe, he concluded, had made a mistake and misapplied the law in his direction to the jury.

Mr McGinn said it was impossible to establish the basis of Judge Roe's decision given that he was now deceased and there was no written ruling of the decision in the case.

While his report put an end to some of the more salacious theories that abounded about the Molloy case, it did not wholly disprove all of them, in particular the 1994 claims of a conflict of interest.

In his review, Mr McGinn found that efforts by Gardaí to locate the Roe letters to the DPP had failed and it had not been possible to stand up Guerin's claims.

The former DPP Eamonn Barnes told Gardaí there was no truth to the suggestion that Judge Roe wrote to him about the trial and neither he nor any member of his staff had any recollection of receiving any such letter.

When members of the Garda Serious Crime Review Team trawled through files relating to the Molloy case at the DPP's Office, they did not find evidence of any correspondence from Judge Roe to the DPP, as claimed by Guerin.

According to the McGinn report, the alleged Roe letters "either never existed, have been destroyed or lost, or otherwise are not available for examination".

Taking into account Mr Barnes' "emphatic denial" of any such correspondence, Mr McGinn said the only evidence of the letters' existence was Guerin's article in the *Sunday Independent*.

His report further confirmed that instead of finding the alleged Roe letters, Gardaí found a handwritten letter about Richard Flynn's trial penned by the prosecution counsel rather than the presiding judge.

"It is possible that a cursory reading of this document could give rise to the assumption that this is a letter handwritten by the judge with a view to explaining his reasoning. It may be the case, therefore, that the article written by Veronica Guerin in 1994 which describes such a letter was based on seeing this document and on the erroneous assumption that Judge Roe had written it," the McGinn report stated.

Family members, however, believe that the letters did exist. Bill Maher, said he had no doubt that the file and letters existed. "I spoke to Veronica Guerin on several occasions and she was adamant about the Molloy file and knew where it was located. I never had any reason to doubt the information she shared," Mr Maher said.

Judge Roe had form for making newspaper headlines, regularly featuring either in the news or racing pages.

He came to national prominence in the 1980s when he was appointed President of the Circuit Court and when some of his rulings were called into question.

While he was not soft on crime, there were several cases before and after the trial of Richard Flynn where his compassion and leniency towards defendants not only raised eyebrows but also angered victims and their families.

Some of his more conservative and controversial rulings also provide an insight into his character, judgement and old-fashioned beliefs, while also reflecting the times we lived in.

The son of a circuit court judge with Fine Gael connections, Judge Roe followed in his father's footsteps to pursue a career in law. He also tried his hand, unsuccessfully, at running for public office in Louth in 1948 and 1951.

After studying law at UCD, where he was both auditor of the Literary and Historical Debating Society and president of the then students' council, he was called to the Bar in 1942 and went on to serve as a District and Circuit Court Judge on the Eastern Circuit.

Aside from law and politics, he spent much of his time pursuing his other passion – horses. When he was not holding court, he attended race meetings, either as a jockey, trainer or racing steward and was well known in horse racing circles.

A member of the Turf Club, Judge Roe had some success on the race track and also took part in national hunt meetings.

In his younger days he steered his horse, My Oul Segocia, home to win the Ulster National in 1965 but gave up jockeying to turn his hand to training in his later years.

In 1983 his horse, Carlingford Castle, netted Stg£68,000 in winnings when it romped home to take second place in the Epsom Derby. The racing judge, as he was sometimes referred to, had purchased the horse at a jockey's dance two years previously for just IR£8,000.

When Fine Gael came to power in a coalition government with Labour in 1973, the Taoiseach Liam Cosgrave offered his old school friend and racing companion a judicial appointment, elevating him from the District Court to the Circuit Court.

In the wake of Cosgrave's resignation in 1977, Roe turned down an opportunity and handsome salary of IR£12,000 to sit as a High Court Judge.

A lifelong bachelor, who also owned a local newspaper in his native county of Louth, Judge Roe liked to think of himself as a man of the people and had a preference for remaining in the countryside, no doubt to maintain his interest in horses.

In February 1986, just months before the trial of Mr Flynn, Judge Roe was appointed by the Garret FitzGerald-led government to President of the Circuit Court, a role that would combine administrative duties and enable him to sit at Chancery Lane in Dublin.

In the first trial since his elevation to Circuit Court President, Judge Roe attracted headlines for branding a new rule on verdicts as a "silly law".

The new Department of Justice regulation, introduced the previous year, required juries to spend at least two hours deliberating a case before reaching a majority verdict.

Judge Roe remarked: "It is a silly law and an insult to a jury. When it was brought in I wrote to the Department saying it was crazy," he told the court.

While he was considered fair, hard-working and a judge who adopted a common-sense approach, Judge Roe was not afraid to ruffle feathers or to go out on a limb, inside or outside the courtroom.

According to State Papers, he asked the government to intervene and support the release from a German prison of the deputy Nazi leader, Rudolf Hess, in the 1970s.

In a letter to then Foreign Affairs Minister Michael O'Kennedy in December 1977, Roe wrote: "This is my Christmas good deed – can you do anything to get unfortunate Rudolf Hess released? AJP Taylor (historian) makes an unanswerable case. I like AJP very much – he is always very favourable to Ireland and the Irish."

He also had no qualms about holding the government or Taoiseach of the day to account on occasion.

In 1980, Judge Roe wrote to the then Taoiseach Charles Haughey complaining of the unfair and differential tax treatment of some judges.

Roe said it was a "scandal" that High Court, Supreme Court, and Dublin Circuit Court judges were allowed higher tax reliefs against their income compared to Circuit Court judges.

He had initially raised the matter, without success, with the Finance Minister Michael O'Kennedy and subsequently sent Haughey two letters highlighting his concerns.

"I would ask you to have a word with Michael and see that justice is done," Judge Roe wrote.

Haughey, who himself had a penchant for the high life, replied: "I am, of course, familiar with your own modest but discriminating lifestyle and your appreciation of haute-cuisine and a fine vintage.

"I hope that whatever the outcome of the grinding of the bureaucratic machine, your impeccable standards may never be lowered."

In the courtroom, Judge Roe's conservative views, often described as "Victorian" in press reports, regularly shone through in his rulings and concluding remarks.

In 1983, he made headlines for advising anyone seeking condoms outside of chemist shop hours to "wait until Monday" to get a prescription.

He was commenting on an appeal by Kildare GP Dr Andrew Rynne, who was convicted of illegally selling condoms to a patient in breach of family planning laws at that time, when condoms were only permitted to be purchased on prescription from a chemist for family planning or medical reasons.

Describing the appeal as a "storm in a tea cup", Judge Roe dismissed the IR£500 fine imposed on Dr Rynne.

He also took the opportunity to urge the Church hierarchy to get back to its "primary duty of helping people lead decent, chaste and pure lives".

"It used to be preached by the Church that people shouldn't indulge in sexual relations outside marriage. Perhaps it might be better, it would at least be one way of dealing with the problem, if the church preached this a little more often," Judge Roe remarked.

"My advice to Dr Rynne is, if people seek condoms, to which they are legally entitled, he should give them a prescription and they should take it to a chemist. If they leave it too late, ask them to wait until Monday," he added.

His comments were met with some amusement at the time and even led to a race horse being named 'Wait until Monday'.

In 1984 Judge Roe ruled in a defamation case involving a former Rose of Tralee and model, Marie Soden, who was awarded IR£2,000 after a magazine portrayed her as someone who would regularly quaff pints of Guinness in a pub.

It was not so much the verdict or payout that drew attention but Judge Roe's outdated remarks at the time: "What could be more defamatory of any woman, young or old, married or single, than to portray her sitting at a bar in this fashion. Who would like to think of their daughter or wife or grandmother like this. Who would want their son to be associated with a girl like that?"

###

Judge Roe's unorthodox intervention in the 1986 trial of Richard Flynn was not the first time that the racing judge attracted headlines.

In 1981 Judge Roe presided over a trial, lasting less than two hours, where a doctor who had shot and killed a man he mistook for a deer walked free from Wicklow Circuit Court.

It was around 5pm in the evening on 22 November 1980 when the doctor, a keen hunter, accidently shot the man, who had been out walking with a companion in Curtlestown Wood, near Enniskerry in Co Wicklow.

The doctor said he saw something black in the woods and thought it was a stag deer and shot at it.

"If I had the slightest reason to suspect that a human being was in the area at this hour, I would not have shot," the doctor told Gardaí.

Once he realised it was not a deer, the doctor attended to the wounded man, 27-year-old Frederick Denham, and took him to hospital but he died on the way. Denham had been shot in the chest with a .22 bolt action rifle.

The court heard that the accused, who pleaded not guilty to a manslaughter charge, was the "pillar of the community and highly respected". The defending counsel submitted that the prosecution had not established a case for manslaughter against the GP, who had pleaded not guilty.

Judge Roe agreed and directed the jury to issue a not guilty verdict. The doctor had made a mistake but this did not amount to criminal negligence, the judge summed up.

"I have no doubt that anyone hearing the evidence in this case must hold that the doctor was not guilty of criminal negligence. The place was lonely, isolated, on a Saturday afternoon in the winter; it was not a place where many people go and he had no reason to think that the figure which emerged was a human being but thought it was a stag. It was a mistake on his part but it does not amount to criminal negligence. For those reasons, I must direct you to bring in a verdict of not guilty," Judge Roe said.

The case led to changes in regulations around hunting with the Department of Forestry banning deer hunting in the evenings, restricting it to before 10.30am, and also banning hunting on Sundays.

In the run-up to the Molloy case and before Judge Roe's ascension to Circuit Court President, he already had form for deviating from the rule of law.

Some of his controversial rulings sparked calls for his resignation or for the establishment of independent inquiries.

In 1983, Judge Roe again made headlines when he handed down a suspended sentence to a drink-driver involved in a horror crash that killed six people.

A jury had found 24-year-old lorry driver John McCloskey, from Mornington in Co Louth, guilty of dangerous driving causing the death of 19-year-old Sheila Nugent, outside Drogheda in February that year.

The defendant had pleaded guilty to leaving the scene of an accident and driving without a tachograph.

McCloskey admitted to consuming seven to eight pints of Guinness throughout the day and attending a function in Bettystown that night. He then drove under the influence, crashing into a minibus carrying youths home from a nearby disco.

The court heard that he was driving at 30 miles per hour when he realised the road was dangerous because of icy conditions. When he passed a slow moving car, his lorry cab went out of control and crashed into the minibus.

The lorry careered through a ditch and became embedded in trees, while the minibus was pushed back 90 feet in the impact of the crash, according to press reports.

When it came to sentencing, Judge Roe handed the lorry driver down a two-year suspended prison sentence and banned him from driving for 15 years.

His ruling led to rebukes and calls for Judge Roe's resignation from the relatives of those who lost their lives in the deadly crash.

Addressing the judge in open court, David Shields, whose 19-year-old sister, Paula, had perished in the minibus, said: "This is a disgrace. I object. You should retire from the bench. You sentenced a man last week to 12 months for stealing sheep and now you let this man off after killing six people."

When Mr Shields was removed from the court by Gardaí, his mother, Gertie Shields, stood up and told the court how she was appalled by the judge's decision.

The defendant had previous convictions for failing to stop at the scene of an accident, failing to report an accident, and driving without insurance among others, the court had heard.

"He killed six people, then went home to bed without caring and played football on Sunday," Mrs Shields told the court.

Judge Roe extended his heartfelt sympathies to the families involved but said he felt the driving ban was a severe sentence in the case.

He decided against jailing McCloskey because, Judge Roe said, the defendant did not intend doing harm to anybody or anything and the road conditions were icy at the time.

Ultimately, the high-profile drink-driving case led to the formation of Mothers Against Drink Drivers, a campaign group set up by Mrs Shields in the wake of the ruling.

Less than eight years later, McCloskey had his driving licence restored, realising Mrs Shields fears. The situation, the drink-driving campaigner told members of the press, made her "absolutely sick".

"I was given an undertaking by Judge Roe at the time that the ban would last the full 15 years. I asked for the undertaking because I was afraid of something like this," she commented.

"This kind of thing makes a mockery of the law," she added.

Judge Roe also presided over a trial in November 1984 in which a 56-year-old married restaurant owner was cleared of allegedly tying up and raping his former lover.

The trial had heard that the 30-year-old qualified midwife, who already had a child by the accused, woke up in her bedroom to find him with a glass of wine in one hand and a revolver in the other.

She was ordered to take off her clothes, and then his, before being forced to have sex against her will. She had also received several blows to the head from the revolver and when she came to, she was bound by a rope at the neck, hands and feet.

The accused, who denied all charges, was cleared of rape and false imprisonment but found guilty, by a jury, of assaulting the woman in her home.

In evidence, the defendant said he had no knowledge of the events and that he had drank a lot of wine.

Describing the case as "very extraordinary and sad", Judge Roe said both parties had suffered greatly but it was clearly not a case for a prison sentence.

Judge Roe said the verdict of the jury represented a humane and common sense view of the case and he hoped that both parties could put the past behind them and go on "to make a better job of their lives".

Another highly contentious trial in 1984, involving the death of a man in custody in a Co Cavan Garda station, sparked calls for an independent inquiry.

The particular case involved the death of 42-year-old, Peter Matthews, who died after allegedly being assaulted in custody at Shercock Garda Station in April 1982.

Matthews, a father of four, was brought to the station for questioning over the alleged theft of a post office book and alleged fraudulent conversion of IR£30 from the account.

Under interrogation, Matthews received head, eye, arm and back injuries, as well as a severe blow to the stomach, which drove his pancreas into his spine. A post-mortem found he died from a heart attack.

The death in custody case involved two separate trials but in the end, nobody was brought to justice for the beating that Matthews suffered prior to his death. Both trials were fraught with conflicting evidence from witnesses, as well as claims that those charged were being scapegoated.

In the first trial in 1983, the Garda Sergeant on duty that night, Sergeant Peter Diviney, was acquitted of a charge of common assault on Matthews and the jury could not agree on a charge of false imprisonment.

In the second prosecution in 1984, Detective Garda Thomas Jordan was cleared of all charges after a sensational three-day trial that heard conflicting statements from his Garda colleagues and other witnesses present on the night.

Judge Roe withdrew manslaughter and false imprisonment charges against Garda Jordan because of a doubt in the evidence while the jury found him not guilty on charges of actual and grievous bodily harm.

The trial heard that Matthews, from Carrickmacross in Monaghan, had suffered a heart attack just months previously and had told Gardaí at the station that he had a heart condition.

The State Pathologist Dr John Harbison said Mathews could have died at any moment due to his bad heart but concluded that his death was due to coronary thrombosis, brought on by the violence meted out to him at the station.

The sergeant in charge and other members present on the night changed their statements a year after Mr Matthews died and told the court they had falsified their earlier statements to protect their Garda colleague before the court.

Initial statements suggested that the death was from natural causes and failed to mention any violence towards the father-of-four but subsequent statements pointed the finger at Garda Jordan, who had attended from another station that night.

Another Garda officer was heard saying that he loved to hear suspects "roaring" just before an unseemly noise was made in the station, the trial was told.

Garda Jordan gave a statement that Matthews was sitting face downwards on a chair when he attended the station and within a short time noted that he appeared to be totally lifeless. He tried to resuscitate Matthews.

The defence counsel, Patrick McEntee SC, submitted that the evidence "would not hang a cat" and that Garda Jordan was being used as a scapegoat.

"There were three sad people so deranged that they no longer knew what was lies and what was the truth, finding themselves in dire trouble," Mr McEntee said.

"They had hunted around for a scapegoat and what better scapegoat than the man from the other station," he added.

In the end, Judge Roe withdrew the charges. Evidence that the deceased had a bad heart was a factor in his ruling.

"I am of the opinion that even if the jury found that the defendant assaulted the deceased, that in view of Dr Harbison's evidence it would be impossible for them to hold that the death was caused by the assault," Judge Roe ruled.

"Dr Harbison's evidence is very clear. The deceased had a bad heart. It could have caused his death at any time. Dr Harbison also stated that, if the deceased died from an assault, the blow or blows would have had to be struck 15 minutes before death. The evidence, if accepted by the jury, of any blows being struck by the defendant is that they were struck a few minutes or seconds before death," he added.

It was not safe to put the case to the jury, Judge Roe said, withdrawing the manslaughter and false imprisonment charges but allowing the assault charges to proceed.

The jury found Garda Jordan not guilty on the remaining assault charges. The verdict caused widespread shock and anger, not least for Anne Mathews, wife of the deceased. "Someone somewhere is going to have to find out the truth," she said. "It is admitted by everyone that Peter was injured in the Garda station. This situation is just not good enough.

"If ordinary members of the public had done something wrong you can be sure it would be sorted out in less than two years. I am totally disgusted with the whole thing."

The lack of answers or justice in the case prompted Mrs Mathews to seek an independent inquiry. "I will have to demand justice one way or the other. There seems to be one law for the Gardaí and another for the public," she said.

Any public disquiet was short-lived, however, as the calls for an inquiry fell on deaf ears at a time when the government of the day was drafting a Criminal Justice Bill to give Gardaí more powers and to provide greater protections for anyone detained in custody.

Remarkably, less than two years later, similar cries for an independent inquiry would be heard in the Molloy case when heart issues were raised as a possible cause of death.

Judge Roe was by no means the only member of the judiciary to court controversy in the 1980s or since then.

Amid calls for greater transparency and accountability from members of the bench, some judges moved to explain their judgments to allay any public concern or disquiet.

Judge Roe, however, never availed of that opportunity in any of the more controversial cases he heard.

The issue was highlighted in an *Irish Times* editorial on 2 July 1986, shortly after Richard Flynn's acquittal.

The editorial drew on other recent high-profile cases, including a 1983 trial that saw a group of Dublin youths walk free after beating up and killing a gay man in Fairview Park and the dropping of a murder charge against double-murderer Malcolm MacArthur in 1984.

"In previous cases judges have seen fit to explain for the benefit of a general public which is not well versed in jurisprudence. Mr Justice Gannon did so after the Fairview Park killing. Mr Justice McMahon did so after the Malcom MacArthur case. The Director of Public Prosecutions saw fit to explain his actions and his policies too. There was no great precedent to prevent Justice Roe speaking up. Quite the contrary," the newspaper editorial stated.

"The independence of the judiciary affords it almost complete protection from criticism. That same protection should oblige it to give account of itself when its decisions seem puzzling to the general public or when they cause concern. If ever there was such a case, this is one," it concluded.

Amid calls for Judge Roe to clarify his decision and ruling in the Flynn trial, he received some support from surprising quarters.

Within days of the *Irish Times* editorial, the *Sunday Press* newspaper carried a glowing tribute to Judge Roe on 6 July 1986 – just shy of a year since Fr Molloy was killed.

The article – 'Galloping Judge Roe' – was written by Conor Lenihan, son of Fianna Fail TD and former Tánaiste and Minister for Justice, Brian Lenihan, a close friend of the Flynn family, who had attended the wedding at Kilcoursey House the previous year.

Despite the family connection, Conor Lenihan, then working as a freelance journalist, wrote an overtly favourable profile that claimed there was "virtually no criticism" of Judge Roe, whose name "immediately evokes expressions of affection in legal circles".

Years later, in 2010, Mr Lenihan, who had by then entered the world of politics, defended the 1986 profile and told the *Irish Independent* he had "absolutely no regrets" about writing the piece.

The former Fianna Fáil TD further told Gardaí in 2011, as part of a fresh examination into the Molloy case, that the *Sunday Press* may have been nervous about potentially defaming a judge and took a different view of Judge Roe compared to other national newspaper titles.

Mr Lenihan told Gardaí he formed his own impressions about Judge Roe having covered Naas Circuit Court for the *Leinster Leader* newspaper one summer and that he had no information to offer in relation to Fr Molloy's death.

Judge Roe retired from the bench in 1990 at the age of 70. He then moved to Kildare to maintain his interest in horses. Up until his death in October 2003, at the age of 83, Judge Roe never publicly commented on the Molloy case again.

While he was described by many in legal circles as industrious, fair and a champion of the common man, his old-fashioned, and at times conservative, view of the world was evident in how he ruled in the courtroom.

Solicitor Ben O'Rafferty, who represented the Molloy family at Niall's inquest, echoes the view that Judge Roe was someone who managed his courtroom well.

"I always found him extremely courteous and efficient and pleasant to deal with, and he ran the Circuit Court in Dublin in a very efficient manner," Mr O'Rafferty said.

He believes, however, that the long-standing judge erred in the Flynn trial when he directed the jury to acquit. "Judge Roe got it wrong at the trial and there should have been a full hearing and the matter put to a jury," he said.

Even after Judge Roe's death the questions persisted about why he had ruled as he did.

The unsolved killing attracted renewed media and public interest when Gardaí mounted a fresh review of the case in 2010.

At a public meeting in Castlecoote in 2013 to bring pressure for a public inquiry, Fianna Fáil Senator Terry Leyden, revealed that he had previously confronted Judge Roe about the controversial ruling.

"I put it to Frank Roe, one to one, 'Why did you acquit Richard Flynn for the murder or manslaughter of Fr Niall Molloy?' And strangely enough he actually was prepared to engage with me. He knew the family involved and should never have taken the case, that's absolutely right," Senator Leyden said at the time.

The Senator further claimed that he raised the case with former Fine Gael TD Michael Noonan, who was Minister for Justice at the time of the priest's death.

"He was told by a TD from Laois/Offaly at the time that no-one ever will stand trial for this murder. I won't name that person now but the Minister told me himself. He was so concerned he went to the Secretary General of the Department of Justice to report what was said to him," Senator Leyden said.

Today, more than 30 years later, Judge Roe's questionable ruling in the Molloy case continues to beg more questions than answers and to cast a shadow over his lengthy career in law.

Chapter 7
THE WAY IT WAS

Ireland in the 1980s was marked by political volatility, concerns over the judicial system, and a fair share of scandals and controversies.

The arrest of murder suspect Malcolm MacArthur in 1982 at the apartment of the then Attorney General Patrick Connolly must go down as one of the most bizarre events of this era.

It was so unfathomable for a suspected double murderer to be found at the apartment of the most senior law officer of the State in the midst of a nationwide manhunt, that the then Taoiseach Charlie Haughey described the circumstances as "grotesque, unbelievable, bizarre and unprecedented" before summoning Mr Connolly, who subsequently resigned.

But it was former Labour TD Conor Cruise O'Brien, a constituency rival of Haughey's, who leapt on the Taoiseach's description of events to coin the term 'GUBU' and use it against him.

"If the situation was GUBU – that is to say grotesque, unbelievable, bizarre and unprecedented – then the greater the credit due to Mr Haughey for dealing with it," Mr O'Brien, an historian and academic, chided in a newspaper column.

The term GUBU stuck and is still used today when questionable events in Irish life occur.

While the 1980s spawned a generation of "young urban professionals" or Yuppies in stronger economies than ours, Ireland was challenged by high unemployment rates that precipitated yet another wave of emigration.

The ongoing Northern Ireland conflict sparked heightened paramilitary activity and terrorist attacks north and south of the border, as well as on the British mainland, but also saw the signing of the Anglo-Irish Agreement in 1985.

On the political front, the 1980s were turbulent to say the least, with as many as five general elections called over the course of the decade, something that has not been repeated since.

The poor economic outlook for the country presented significant challenges and led to swingeing budget cuts and tax hikes, which inevitably brought a number of governments to heel.

In 1982, plans to introduce a hefty 18% VAT rate on children's shoes and clothing led to the budget being voted down and ultimately the collapse of the Fine Gael and Labour coalition government.

Aside from The Troubles and economic and political instability, the period was also heavily influenced by the continued dominance of the Catholic Church, which shaped how we lived, from what we learned at school, to how we worked, to how we planned or raised a family.

In 1985, a marquee erected in the private grounds of a grand house for a lavish family wedding of over 200 guests was almost unheard of; it was a rare event.

For a priest to be found dead in a couple's bedroom at the end of the weekend was even more astonishing and brought the spectre of scandal for the Church.

The first-ever papal visit to Ireland was a momentous occasion and enraptured the nation in 1979. More than 2.5 million worshippers – around 75% of the entire population – turned out to pray with Pope John Paul II during a three-day visit that autumn.

Hundreds of thousands, both young and old, flocked to events across the country, from the Phoenix Park in Dublin to the monastic site in Clonmacnoise and beyond. Fr Niall Molloy was among the many clergy, who celebrated the Pope's visit to Knock Shrine.

The visit came at a time when the church and Vatican was warning against a rise in materialism or a "moral permissiveness", in other words an appetite to enjoy greater freedoms in all aspects of our lives.

"The most sacred principles, which were the sure guides for the behaviour of individuals and society, are being hollowed-out by false pretences concerning freedom, the sacredness of life, the indissolubility of marriage, the true sense of human sexuality, the right attitude towards the material goods that progress has to offer. Many people now are tempted to self-indulgence and consumerism, and human identity is often defined by what one owns," Pope John Paul II said in his homily in the Phoenix Park.

The Pope's visit on the eve of the 1980s is reflective of the times we lived in. It was an era when Ireland continued to command one of the highest Mass attendance rates in Europe – 87% of Irish

Catholics attended Sunday Mass in 1985 and a high proportion also attended additional Masses during the week.

The papal visit set the scene for a new decade in which the Catholic hierarchy would face a raft of challenges and threats, from attempts to introduce divorce and abortion, to the relaxation of access to contraceptives, to a drift away from the church by younger people.

In 1983 a referendum on abortion led to the eighth amendment protecting the life of the unborn, which has since been repealed, and in 1986 a majority of the electorate sided with the church to denounce the notion of divorce.

In both referendums, the Church came out fighting to maintain its grip on the moral conscience of the nation. The influence of the church, while loosening to some extent, remained deep and pervasive at the time.

In March 1985, in the midst of legislative proposals to widen the availability of contraceptives, the Catholic Bishops issued a pastoral letter on love, sex and marriage to reinforce church teachings.

Carried by some national newspapers and read out at Masses across the country, the pastoral highlighted the sanctity of marriage versus the grave sin of sex or pregnancy outside wedlock or the use of contraceptives, which were only available by prescription to married couples.

A new law liberalising the availability of contraceptives was ultimately carried that year prompting some to suggest that the Church-state relationship was no longer as intimate as it once was, but the referendum results and actions of citizens told a different story.

Hundreds of concerned citizens wrote to the then President Patrick Hillery urging him not to sign the new legislation making contraceptives more widely available. A year later, almost two in three voters rejected proposals to legislate for divorce.

In 1985 the country was also gripped by another sacred phenomenon – the spectacle and promise of religious statues moving and speaking in towns and villages across the country.

From the first sighting of a moving statue in Asdee in rural Kerry, the phenomenon spread to Ballinspittle in Co Cork and beyond and from there attracted national and international attention.

As the 'moving statues' mania took hold, people flocked in their droves to Marian grottos around the country to pray and sing, sometimes around the clock, in all-night vigils.

Even though the Church itself did not lend much credence to the sightings, the hysteria surrounding the 'moving statues' reflected a deep devotion and deference towards the Catholic Church at that time.

Overwhelmingly Catholic, the country remained strongly conservative as the Church continued to dominate in many aspects of our lives.

This was still a time when school teacher Eileen Flynn lost her job for living with and getting pregnant by a separated man (1982), when a Church-run hospital refused to provide cancer drugs to a pregnant mother, Sheila Hodgers, in order to protect the life of the unborn (1983) and when Garda Majella Moynihan was pushed out of the force for giving birth outside wedlock (1984).

It was still a time when children and young people continued to be locked away in industrial schools, Magdalene laundries, and mother and baby homes, and when children born outside wedlock had the legal status of being 'illegitimate' right up until 1987 when the law was finally changed.

The Catholic virtues of 'no sex before marriage', the restricted use of contraception, and the criminalisation of homosexuality and of suicide were within the social norms of 1980s Ireland.

From what we know now, this threshold of purity and piety was at odds with the real workings of the Church, which had covered up clerical sex abuse and had a hand in other transgressions, such as illegal adoptions and the abuse and mistreatment of adults and children in a range of residential facilities run by religious orders.

At the time though, as the supreme keeper of virtue, the Church managed to hold sway and deflect any controversy or scandal and keep it under wraps for several more years.

Against the fraught economic and political backdrop of the 1980s, there were growing fears around rising crime rates and concerns over the fairness and effectiveness of the criminal justice system.

By 1983 the number of recorded crimes across the country breached the 100,000 mark but showed signs of tailing off thereafter.

While much of the crime wave stemmed from joyriding youths and a rise in armed crimes, the number of homicides remained relatively stable at between 20-26 per annum in the early 1980s.

According to the official crime report, Gardaí recorded 25 murders in 1985, seven of which remained unsolved at the end of the year.

In one unsolved case the body of a man, with gunshot wounds, was found in a bedroom at his home in Donnybrook, Dublin; in another the body of a woman, with severe head injuries, was found in an upstairs bedroom of her home at Sandycove, Dublin. There were other open cases involving women who had been strangled to death in Kilkenny and Limerick.

The number of manslaughter cases, many relating to road traffic accidents, also ebbed and flowed during this period, ranging from between four to 15 per annum.

Between 1980 and 1985, there were at least seven murder cases where the perpetrators were detected but no criminal proceedings followed, according to official records of that time.

By 1985, the apparent crime wave across the country led to pressure on the network of prisons. Described by the then Justice Minister Michael Noonan as an "emergency", it necessitated the opening of Spike Island as an additional detention facility later that year.

The decade also saw new criminal justice legislation introduced to strengthen Garda powers of detention, provide a mechanism to deal with complaints against Gardaí, and to provide greater protection for anyone held in custody.

Up until the introduction of the 1984 Criminal Justice Act, Gardaí had limited powers of arrest and detention, which were restricted to certain offences under the Offences against the State Act.

New powers enacted in 1987 gave Gardaí the power to arrest and detain individuals suspected of committing serious crimes, where they previously could only invite suspects to help them with their enquiries.

New custody regulations around how Gardaí detained suspects came on the back of several allegations of undue force being used by Gardaí in some instances.

Academic estimates suggest that 23 people died in Garda custody between 1975 and 1983.

At the time, there were also widespread concerns over the rule of law.

In 1985 a landmark report by the National Economic and Social Council (NESC) critiqued the criminal justice system for the first time and recommended sweeping changes and reform.

The wide-ranging report, published in February that year, suggested that 50% of arrests did not lead to prosecutions because of Gardaí using their discretionary power – a claim rejected by the force.

It recommended the formal recording of information on the arrest and charge of individuals and reasons why prosecutions were dropped and called for the role of the Director of Public Prosecutions (DPP) and State Solicitor's Office to be expanded to manage the prosecution of serious offences instead of Gardaí.

The 200-plus page report further recommended 'on the job' training for Garda recruits and also highlighted staffing deficiencies within the system, in particular in the "meagre allocation of personnel and expenditure" to the Office of the Director of Public Prosecutions and the courts service.

The Association of Garda Sergeants and Inspectors (AGSI) rejected the claims about Gardaí using discretionary powers and stressed that the DPP was responsible for pursuing prosecutions.

"Statistics should be made available on the number of cases sent by the Gardaí to the DPP and the number which he subsequently proceeds with. Reasons for not proceeding with some charges should be explained," the AGSI General Secretary said at the time.

If reform was needed in the criminal justice system, he added, it was needed in the Office of the DPP and the legal profession. The report came in the wake of concerns, dating back to the 1970s, about the administration of criminal justice.

Some of these concerns related to claims of a 'Heavy Gang' within the Gardaí, who allegedly used brute force to interrogate suspects and elicit apparently voluntary confessions from innocent citizens of the State.

In 2022 a three-part RTE documentary series *Crimes and Confessions* revisited some of the more high-profile cases, including the investigation into the disappearance of Una Lynskey (1971), the Sallins Train Robbery (1976), and the Kerry Babies scandal (1984) – the 'Heavy Gang' being the common link across all three.

While the wrongful convictions were subsequently overturned, nobody enquired as to how they came about in the first place, despite the fact that several individuals served time for offences they did not commit. Decades later and questions still remain over the rule of law at the time.

In July 1986, the Garda Complaints Bill was signed into law and led to the establishment, for the first time, of a board that would manage grievances from members of the public.

In its first three years of operation, from 1987 to 1989, the Garda Complaints Board handled more than 2,500 complaints, with almost one-third deemed inadmissible. The bulk of complaints (90%) related to allegations of abuse of authority, discourtesy and discreditable conduct. The Board was replaced in 2007 by the Garda Siochána Ombudsman Commission, which today has limited powers to investigate former members. A new more robust and independent police ombudsman has been proposed.

###

The workings of the DPP and how members of the judiciary ruled in cases also came under the spotlight in the 1980s.

In certain high-profile cases, the Office of the DPP was asked to explain why charges were dropped or why it did not proceed with some charges before the court.

The issue came to a head in 1983 when the family of Offaly farmer Donal Dunne, who was murdered the previous year, questioned why charges had been dropped against Malcolm MacArthur.

MacArthur was given a life sentence for the murder of Meath nurse Bridie Gargan in 1982 but had charges of murdering Mr Dunne, possessing a shotgun, and aggravated burglary, dropped.

The decision by the DPP elicited great upset and outrage for the Dunne family, who sought answers.

Christy Dunne, a brother of the deceased farmer, said: "It annoys me greatly that the whole issue of my brother being murdered could be swept away in two minutes in court. I feel the DPP failed to discharge his duties as the Gardaí told me that they had a very comprehensive Book of Evidence. I was totally shocked in court."

"I will never come to terms with his death until somebody is tried. I won't let it rest," he added.

There were also questions around the dropping of charges in relation to the murder of mother and daughter Margaret and Anne Nolan at their Co Wicklow farmhouse in November 1985. Brian Fortune, aged 18, entered a plea agreement that saw him sentenced to life in prison for murdering Margaret Nolan but a second charge for the murder of her daughter was dropped.

In a rare in-depth press interview given by the DPP in 1986, Mr Barnes moved to deflect any criticism of his Office or the need to explain its decisions.

Mr Barnes told the *Irish Press* that the controversy surrounding his decision to drop the charge of murdering Donal Dunne in the MacArthur case was "highly artificial" and asserted that there were "no dark secrets" in his Office.

He repeated that he could not comment on individual cases but pointed out that there was precedent in other double murder cases where his Office did not proceed on one of the murder charges.

The MacArthur controversy, he said, had been "skilfully whipped" up and resulted in "enormous harm" to his Office.

"It is a very serious thing to erode public confidence in the administration of the law unless there is just cause for so doing. In fact the decision in that case could hardly have been more straightforward and self-evident. I doubt if there is anyone who could look me in the eye and seriously say that, on reflection, he or she does not know the reason for my action in that case," Mr Barnes told the *Irish Press*.

In previous weeks, the Dáil Committee on Crime, Lawlessness and Vandalism had called into question some recent decisions of the DPP and suggested that several decisions should be explained to the High Court.

Chair of the Committee, Fianna Fáil TD Michael Woods, said: "There should be a procedure whereby an aggrieved person has a right to appeal a decision made by the DPP."

Responding to such concerns, Mr Barnes said he would welcome some formula that would facilitate his Office explaining certain decisions but further cautioned that the truth could be inconvenient for some.

"There are no dark secrets in this Office. I would be quite happy to throw open the files to any appropriate authority such as the Attorney General or the Minister for Justice or any other designated authority but I cannot open them to the public. To do so would in many cases cause serious injustice," Mr Barnes said.

"I'm afraid that in some cases it might not please some of the people who have been calling most loudly for explanations, the truth can often be very inconvenient," he continued.

"If the real reason a person was not prosecuted became known there might be a lot of sore heads around the country."

Within months, the Dáil committee on Crime, Lawlessness and Vandalism mooted the idea that an all-party subcommittee could monitor decisions and recommendations made by DPP's Office.

A year later, the committee published its final report, which made several recommendations to address "a major and growing concern" about how certain criminal cases were prosecuted.

"There is a need for some mechanism to be established whereby the public can be assured that the decisions of the DPP are not beyond scrutiny," the committee report stated.

To allay public concern in certain cases, such as the MacArthur case, it proposed that decisions could be explained via the Attorney General, the courts service, or possibly a legislative committee.

The Dáil committee also recommended the establishment of an independent prosecution system, which would be led by the DPP and assume responsibility for prosecuting all criminal offences, thus limiting the role of Gardaí.

It further recommended extensive changes to update criminal laws, many of which had not changed for decades. "One of the most serious and basic anomalies concerns the area of powers of arrest... the anomalous position arises, for example, in that a

Garda can arrest for a minor larceny, but not for assault occasioning actual bodily harm, indecent assault or, indeed, attempted rape," the report noted.

The recommendations, however, failed to precipitate change following the dissolution of the committee and a change of government that spring.

Such questions about why charges were dropped or did not proceed were not confined to serious criminal cases involving murder but were also raised when two men were acquitted on vandalism charges for defacing a holy statue in Ballinspittle amidst the 'Moving Statues' period.

In March 1986, the Dáil Committee on Crime, Lawlessness and Vandalism wrote to the Garda Commissioner and DPP seeking an explanation for the defective summons that ultimately led to the accused men walking free from court.

It was some time before legislation was introduced to address some of these issues and enhance victims' rights. The 2017 Criminal Justice (Victims of Crime) Act, for the first time, gave victims the right to seek an explanation from the DPP or Gardaí for non-prosecutions or for a review of such decisions. It was introduced on foot of an EU Directive.

In 1985 there were concerns too over the ability of the DPP's Office, which had only been established a decade earlier, to manage an expanding workload and volume of cases.

In the spring of that year, just months before Fr Molloy's death, a District Court Judge voiced concerns over delays in the DPP's Office, which had led to dozens of cases being struck out.

The judge's comments sparked off a very public spat between members of the judiciary and the DPPs Office.

"I'm sick, sore and tired of requests for remands in cases where the DPP was to serve a Book of Evidence on defendants and endlessly sought more time to do so," District Court Judge Sean Delap remarked in open court.

"The courts are being blamed for these delays and it is not the fault of the courts. It's the DPP's fault and the courts aren't going to take the blame any longer," he added.

While the DPP rebuked Justice Delap's comments as "grossly and unjustly offensive" to his team, he conceded that his Office was short of staff which left it open to a potential "major catastrophe".

Mr Barnes pointed out that it was not the function of the DPP to prepare books of evidence and its function related to giving a direction on a Book of Evidence.

The Office of the DPP, he said, had five legal assistants who each dealt with 1,200-1,400 files annually.

The Chief State Solicitor's Office, which prepared the books of evidence, had 23 staff available but even at this level it remained understaffed.

Weeks later, Justice Delap remained unrepentant for his comments and said that delays in furnishing a Book of Evidence had led to seven to eight cases being struck out at each sitting.

"The hierarchy is trying to wash its hands of the matter but the DPP is the man ultimately responsible and the buck must stop somewhere," the District Court Judge said.

"The duty of the Government is to service the courts and to see that court work is carried out," Judge Delap added.

Another District Court Judge, Hubert Wine, echoed the concerns over delays and remarked that his judicial colleagues were "fed up with remand after remand".

The situation escalated when months later a suspect charged with the fatal stabbing of a 25-year-old Dublin man, George Owens, in May 1985, had the case struck out because the Book of Evidence had not been furnished by a DPP-appointed barrister.

According to press reports, the number of solicitors employed at the DPP's Office plummeted from 14 to five due to a recruitment embargo on public service staff.

At the time, staff shortages were evident in the Office of the DPP, the Attorney General and the Chief State Solicitor.

The lack of resources was also noted in a memo by the Office of the Attorney General in advance of a meeting with the DPP that year. Documents from the national archives show that staff shortages, "restructuring proposals" and "responsibility and answerability for conduct of prosecutions" were among the issues listed for discussion.

An internal memo from the AG's Office stated: "Consideration of the Cinderella approach to the legal services of the State as compared to other areas."

The memo also suggested the need to structure how the DPP and Attorney General liaised on matters of criminal law reform: "From the point of view of the DPP's Office, it is strongly felt that if the Attorney General had responsibility for criminal law reform, or at least a much greater input into it on the policy and creative side, we would improve both the quality and speed of necessary change in this area."

Later that year, Justice Wine remarked that the situation had improved after the message had finally gotten through.

By autumn, the Chief State Solicitor insisted there were no longer undue delays after the government sanctioned the recruitment of 15 additional staff for his Office that year.

In any event, a man was subsequently tried and convicted of manslaughter in the Owens case and jailed for five years in prison.

Despite the case going ahead, however, there were questions later over why a female accomplice was not charged for their part in his death.

The Owens family were aggrieved at the DPP's decision to drop charges against the woman and mounted a lengthy campaign seeking clarification.

Speaking to a national newspaper two years after her brother died, Pauline Cole said the family felt let down by the justice system: "It's hard to make sense of a system which appears to us to have so little regard for human life and human feelings that they do not proceed to prosecute somebody who may have been involved in the taking of an innocent life."

During this period, there were also questions over decisions made by judges at trial or in handing down sentences.

In 1982 Professor of Criminal Law at Trinity College Dublin, Mary McAleese, who would years later be elected President of Ireland, raised concerns over the erratic sentencing practices evident in Irish courts.

Her concerns followed the "simply outrageous" sentencing of a petty criminal to 12 years in prison for a robbery. "The court is brought into disrepute by uneven sentences," she said at the time.

The harsh sentence was contrasted with more lenient rulings, such as three years' prison for kicking a man with intellectual disabilities to death and two years' jail for killing two people in an arson attack.

Another high-profile court case in 1983 involved the killing of a gay man in Fairview Park on the northside of Dublin by a group of youths, who described themselves as "queer bashers".

The teenagers, aged 14 to 19, were convicted of manslaughter but all walked free for their role in the savage beating and death of Declan Flynn the previous year.

Handing down suspended sentences, Mr Justice Seán Gannon said the case did not amount to murder and the youths would serve their sentences if they got into trouble again.

"Unfortunately, it has transpired from the evidence that this was not an isolated incident, but hopefully it will be the last. Everybody is entitled to have feelings and opinions but it should never reach the stage of expressing violence to others," Justice Gannon said, adding that "no element of correction" was required and that all of the youths came from good homes.

The decision not to jail the youths led to calls for Justice Gannon's dismissal, as well as robust debate on the floor of the Dáil.

Fianna Fáil justice spokesman Deputy Michael Woods said: "In this instance, five young men, acting as a gang, admitted to attacking and robbing numerous people in Fairview Park over a number of months last summer. They also admitted beating and robbing a young man which resulted in his death. The suspended sentences of one to four years have led to widespread concern.

"The tragic case in Fairview demands urgent action from the Minister for Justice and the Government. The Minister must first review and assess this case and its implications and then take urgent action."

His party colleague Bertie Ahern, who would years later lead the country as Taoiseach before falling from grace, added: "If the judge concerned had reasons for making his decision he has a public obligation to let us know the reasons. This case has led to far too much disquiet."

The handing down of suspended sentences in the Fairview case was also contrasted with a 12-month jail term for an unemployed man who stole a purse and IR£20 cash.

Fine Gael TD Liam Skelly said: "There is a need for legislation to ensure the avoidance of hit-and-miss justice which can and does occur in the courts."

Justice Minister Michael Noonan, however, reiterated that the justice system was independent from government and he could not see how legislation could assist in making sentences more uniform.

For Declan Flynn's grief-stricken family the outcome of the case was horrifying. "I had expected that justice would be done and seen to be done," Christopher Flynn, Declan's father, said at the time.

The gay community were also concerned and saddened by the lenient sentences handed down.

Activist and rights campaigner David Norris warned that the outcome of the case appeared to give vigilante groups a free hand to intimidate gay people. "It could be interpreted as a licence to kill," he told the *Irish Times*.

The National Gay Federation added: "While we appreciate the limitations of the Irish penal system, we are dismayed and annoyed at the obvious double standards employed in this case and we feel the assailants would not have got off quite so lightly if the particular sexual orientation of the victim had not been made an issue."

There was more controversy to come. In 1984 the discovery of infant remains at two different locations in Co Kerry led to one of the most controversial Garda investigations ever carried out.

Over the past three decades, the Kerry Babies case has exposed how some elements of the criminal justice system functioned in 1980s Ireland.

The case led to wrongful arrests and charges, concerns over the Garda investigation, and a 77-day tribunal of inquiry that made incorrect findings of wrongdoing that were quashed 36 years later.

The Kerry Babies inquiry was set up to investigate how Joanne Hayes and her family confessed to the murder of a newborn baby, found with multiple stab wounds, on a beach at Cahirsiveen, Co Kerry in April 1984.

The Hayes family withdrew their statements to Gardaí and, in October 1984, all charges were dropped.

Ms Hayes was wrongly implicated in the death of the Cahirsiveen baby and her own son while her family were accused of concealing the birth of a child.

The 24-year-old had given birth to a baby boy, who died of natural causes shortly after childbirth and was buried on the family farm in Abbeydorney.

Despite the two infants having different blood groups, Gardaí alleged they were twins and put forward a theory of "superfecundation" in which the babies were conceived by Ms Hayes but fathered by two different men.

While the tribunal established that Hayes was not the mother of the Cahirsiveen baby and had no responsibility for the infant's death, it wrongfully concluded that she had killed her newborn son.

Decades later, DNA tests in 2018 further ruled Ms Hayes out as the mother of the Cahersiveen baby and led to a fresh probe being launched by Gardaí.

Since then, Ms Hayes and her family have received State apologies and compensation, as well as legal declarations quashing a series of unfounded and incorrect findings of wrongdoing made by the tribunal in 1985.

In May 1986, dozens of citizens, worn down and disillusioned by the legal and criminal justice system, came together to form the National Legal Justice Action Group.

The action group's platform was to campaign for an independent ombudsman for the legal profession, to provide an alternative avenue of complaint to the Law Society, which was the only option available at the time.

Among those who signed up to the new action group were the families of Fr Niall Molloy and Patrick Nugent, who were brought together through death and tragedy.

Both families had lost a loved one in suspicious circumstances but were left without answers.

Patrick Nugent was found dead, aged 23, on the grounds of Bunratty Castle and Folk Park in February 1984. He had been working as a banqueting manager and attending to a wedding anniversary party of more than 50 people, which included two off-duty Gardaí.

There were allegations of a row breaking out and a car striking Mr Nugent but the full facts never emerged despite a subsequent manslaughter trial, inquest and internal Garda inquiries.

Through this new action group, both families united in grief, anger, and a quest for justice.

Fr Molloy's brother, Billy, at one stage considered a run for the Dáil on the NLJAG platform, as did members of the Nugent family.

The justice group ran a number of Dáil candidates in Wicklow, Limerick and Tipperary in the 1987 and 1989 general elections, including Martin Nugent, a brother of Patrick, and Barbara Hyland, from Bray in Wicklow, and Donal Kealy, from Nenagh in Tipperary, who also had axes to grind with the justice system.

Just days before the Molloy inquest opened in July 1986, the justice group lashed out at the then Justice Minister Alan Dukes for failing to act on complaints of alleged abuses by solicitors. "We are furious. The Minister has completely ignored us in our demands for justice and action," Mr Kealy remarked.

Later that year, the action group organised a protest outside Dáil Eireann and the Four Courts over how the Molloy and Nugent cases were handled.

In a letter carried by the *Sunday Independent*, Mr Kealy said the group, which included Molloy and Nugent family members, felt "there is no justice in Irish courts" and that many families had suffered as a result. "Does money overrule justice in Ireland today? Is there a law for the rich and the poor? These are the key questions," he wrote.

Decades later, both the Molloy and Nugent families had their hopes raised when the government of the day agreed to review the unsolved deaths.

For the Nugent family, the case was granted a Section 42 inquiry under the 2005 Garda Síochána Act.

The case featured among hundreds of complaints and grievances considered by a government-led independent review process in 2014, and was one of just five cases to be granted an inquiry.

In 2021, former judge Patrick Clyne concluded his inquiry into the case and shared his findings with the Nugent family, but only on the basis that they signed a confidentiality agreement.

The Clyne Report, which has not been published to date, found that the original Garda investigation was inadequate and recommended a cold case investigation.

Deirdre Nugent, who is married to Patrick's brother, John, said the family were pushing for an independent investigation of Patrick's death by an external policing agency or a full commission of investigation.

"We don't want the Gardaí anywhere near this. We want an external policing agency from another jurisdiction to independently investigate Pat's death or a public inquiry," Deirdre said.

"It is coming up to 40 years and Pat's brothers, John and Martin, feel like they are back at square one. It is not right for families of victims to have to go knocking on the door, begging for justice. It is unbelievable really," she added.

The Molloy case followed a different path, one that involved a fresh Garda probe mounted in 2010 followed by a legal review of all facts in the case. The fresh examination of the 1985 killing, however, did not have a satisfactory conclusion for the Molloys.

"Like the Nugent family, we still do not have answers or justice almost four decades later," Bill Maher said.

PART B

THE EVIDENCE THEN AND NOW

Chapter 8
COLD CASE REVIEW AND MCGINN REPORT

More than two decades after Fr Niall Molloy's killing, two key changes brought some fresh hope for the Molloy family.

Within An Garda Siochána, a new cold case unit called the Serious Crime Review Team (SCRT) was created in 2007, as well as a new body to deal with complaints about policing, the Garda Siochána Ombudsman Commission (GSOC).

Once established, Fr Molloy's relatives approached both the cold case unit and GSOC to press for the case to be reopened.

Around the same time, some media outlets, such as the *Irish Independent*, began to take a new interest in the case. This resurrected the deep feelings of unease and public disquiet that had long surrounded Fr Molloy's death and also led to allegations of a "cover-up" resurfacing.

Nothing came of the approaches to GSOC at the time, but in late 2010, after the Molloy family had been engaging with the SCRT in the background, the outgoing Garda Commissioner Fachtna Murphy announced a review of the cold case.

It was made clear that the fresh probe did not amount to a full re-investigation of Fr Molloy's death but the SCRT, led by Chief

Superintendent Christopher Mangan, was directed to reassess the evidence and re-interview witnesses.

While Richard Flynn could never be retried for the manslaughter or assault of Fr Molloy, Gardaí hoped to at least obtain some answers for the priest's family, who had been left in the dark for decades about how Niall had died.

Over the next two and a half years, the team of senior Gardaí spoke to dozens of potential witnesses, although many declined to offer any new information.

By 2010, several key witnesses had also passed away, including Therese Flynn, Dr Daniel O'Sullivan and Fr James Deignan.

While the cold case review did not yield definitive answers, it is understood it did make a recommendation for a Commission of Investigation into Fr Molloy's death. Such an inquiry could compel witnesses to give evidence under oath.

Chief Superintendent Mangan knew he faced considerable limitations and challenges but remained hopeful of getting a break in the case.

However, given the death of several witnesses and the fact that other key individuals could not be compelled to speak to Gardaí about what happened in Kilcoursey House that weekend, the breakthrough failed to materialise.

"We obtained a certain amount of answers for the Molloy family but they have a lot of questions that remain unanswered," the Chief Superintendent said.

While some people engaged with the SCRT, including one member of the Flynn family, others did not.

When approached by Gardaí, 25 years on, several witnesses referred the SCRT back to their original statements made in 1985 and by law they were within their rights to do so. They were under no legal obligation to comment further to Gardaí.

By this stage, Mr Flynn's health was failing and his doctor confirmed that he was "physically and mentally unable" to under-go any questioning by SCRT members.

This was "unfortunate", Chief Superintendent Mangan said: "I had wanted to engage with him to see, even if after all these years, that he might provide some answers for Fr Molloy's family."

On completing the SCRT review and going as far as they could, Gardaí shared their findings with the Director of Public Prosecutions for consideration.

In August 2013, however, the DPP advised that no new charges or prosecutions could be brought on foot of the two-year Garda review.

The Molloy family were once again crestfallen but determined to step up their campaign for an independent commission of investigation.

"Now is the time for politicians to indicate which way they are going to go. I think that, individually, there is quite a bit of support but what would concern me is that the party line could be taken and scupper any chances of getting an investigation," Henry McCourt, a nephew of Fr Molloy's, told the *Roscommon Herald*, when the outcome was first revealed.

"There is so much in this sad and sorry case that it's very important to have an investigation; there are many important questions that need to be answered from a civilised society point of view," he added.

Despite the family's obvious disappointment, the SCRT exercise did yield some answers as Gardaí were able to establish certain facts and dispel several myths that had flourished over the years.

There was no question over the extent of the personal and business relationship between Fr Molloy and the Flynns over the years.

"Niall had his own room at Kilcoursey House and was considered almost part of the Flynn family," Chief Superintendent Mangan said.

It was also undisputed that Niall had died in "very violent circumstances" as a result of a serious assault but several questions remained over the timeline of events and the true motive behind the apparent bedroom row.

"We endeavoured to try and see if we could fill in those gaps, we were unable to do so because we didn't obtain new statements from anybody who was actually there at the scene," Chief Superintendent Mangan said.

The cold case review by Gardaí also put to bed some of the more sensational claims and rumours that circulated about Niall's death and the events that followed.

Chief Superintendent Mangan accepted that allegations of a "cover-up" and conspiracy theories came to light after Judge Roe's extraordinary intervention at the 1986 trial but said his team were able to debunk some of the myths that persisted.

One particularly distasteful claim was that Fr Molloy had been mutilated or castrated, which Chief Superintendent Mangan rebutted as a "complete falsehood".

Over the years, there were also claims that another party, not Mr Flynn, was responsible for Fr Molloy's death, although the SCRT could not find any evidence to support such claims.

Some witnesses proffered conversations and "hearsay" as evidence but Chief Superintendent Mangan stressed that such information did not stand up as fact and could not be used before a court of law.

While there were claims of other individuals being present at Kilcoursey House on the night that Fr Molloy was beaten and died, Gardaí to date have not been able to verify these claims.

There have also been rumours that a row occurred downstairs or possibly even in an outdoor stable, and that the priest's body was then brought upstairs to the master bedroom, but again these claims have not been substantiated to date.

There were also conflicting accounts of conversations about what transpired days before, and on the night Fr Molloy died.

One witness, a local man, informed Gardaí that a friend, who had worked for the Flynns, told him that he had been present at Kilcoursey on the night and observed events – a claim that was flatly denied by this individual when they spoke to SCRT members.

The local man also told Gardaí in 2012 that his friend spoke of an incident at Kilcoursey House on the Thursday night before the wedding, which had then spilled over into Sunday – again a claim that has to date not been corroborated.

In an interview as part of the documentary, Chief Superintendent Mangan said he believed that Fr Molloy and Richard and Therese Flynn were the only individuals present in the bedroom that night when events unfolded and only they could reveal what happened, but unfortunately they were all now deceased.

"I have had no direct testimony from any other person who would put somebody else present in the room and causing the death of Fr Niall Molloy. I simply have no evidence of it," he said.

In so far as they could, Gardaí examined the business dealings between the Flynns and Fr Molloy but were hampered by the loss of crucial banking and financial documents over the years.

They confirmed that the business partnership mainly involved the purchase and sale of horses and cattle and that Niall had wished to disentangle himself from these dealings prior to his death – information that was already known to Gardaí in 1985.

Gardaí believe that Fr Molloy paid over a sizeable deposit – anywhere from IR£11,000 to IR£24,000 – to Mr Flynn in 1984 for land at Kilcoursey.

They could not, however, verify the amount the priest had paid over to his long-standing friend or if the deposit was returned after that land deal collapsed, just months before Niall's death.

Having corroborated some of the business dealings and trans-actions between the priest and the Flynns, Gardaí, like the Molloy family, were left with even more questions than answers.

"A lot of money had not been properly accounted for. Was that a motive for killing Fr Molloy at the time? Was that a motive for the disagreement that obviously did take place in the bedroom on that night?" Chief Superintendent Mangan said.

"How could a row escalate into the death of Fr Niall Molloy in the bedroom? What was going on? What were the business dealings? Those remain very unanswered questions," he added.

"I tell you what I know happened from the evidence. That's all I can do."

###

Although information gathered as part of the SCRT process did not yield a breakthrough in the Molloy case, it did raise questions about the criminal trial and original investigation.

When the case returned to the media spotlight from 2010 onwards, the Molloy family made renewed calls for a full Commission of Investigation.

The case was once again gaining traction and pressure was building, in the press and within political circles, to secure justice and answers for Fr Molloy's relatives.

Under the 2004 Commissions of Investigation Act, a government minister can seek the support of the Dáil to "investigate any matter considered by the Government to be of significant public concern".

At local and national level, politicians from all parties pledged their support for a Commission of Investigation, in particular in the run-up to the 2011 general election.

Considerable support also came from Fr Molloy's parish of Castlecoote and from those who knew him.

In a letter to Fine Gael Justice Minister Alan Shatter, a retired clergyman and former friend of Niall urged the Minister to sanction a public inquiry into the case.

Borrowing a quote from Dr Martin Luther King, Fr Frank McGauran wrote that "injustice anywhere is a threat to justice everywhere".

"I have not the least doubt that there is no other way of getting to the truth of this grave matter without fear or favour. In my view justice must be seen to be done," Fr McGauran said.

"Unless and until this does happen, the widespread unease, distrust and suspicion of cover-up and collusion at a high level will inevitably fester and grow deeper," he added.

In a bid to quell growing public unrest around the case, Minister Shatter announced his intention to commission an independent review of the cold case, which he hoped would dispel any "baseless assertions" that the government was attempting to suppress information about the case.

"Wider concerns have, of course, been expressed about the case including claims that it has been subject to some sort of cover-up by the State. Against that background, I am anxious to put as much information into the public domain about this matter as is possible and appropriate so as to address these claims," Minister Shatter said.

By Christmas 2013, Minister Shatter appointed a legal expert, Senior Counsel Dominic McGinn, to independently examine what Gardaí had unearthed in the SCRT exercise.

While the Molloy family gave the review a cautious welcome and harboured some concerns over the terms of reference, they clung tightly to the possibility that a public inquiry could finally become a reality.

Local politicians also expressed concern over the extent and scope of the review, with Labour Senators John Kelly and John Whelan calling for a full public inquiry. "This appointment of a Senior Counsel appears on paper to be no more than somebody who is, again, trawling over the same paperwork that the DPP and the Minister himself have previously trawled over," the senators for Roscommon and Laois/Offaly said in a joint statement.

Two years later, however, any hopes of a public inquiry were dashed when Mr McGinn published his findings on 31 March 2015.

The Molloy family was given scant notice that the 109-page report was being published that afternoon and was left scrambling to ascertain its conclusion before it went public.

The report came with a proviso – that it sought to identify any issues of public interest warranting further inquiry or that could help to establish the truth but it was spelled out in explicit terms that it did not seek to establish the truth or venture an opinion.

On reviewing the SCRT file, the senior counsel came to the conclusion that any real prospect of getting to the truth was eroded by the passage of time.

"While there are a number of issues of public interest which have been identified and enumerated, some of which could be categorised as issues of significant public interest or concern, it is unlikely given the passage of time, the death of many of the pertinent witnesses and the reluctance of others voluntarily to give evidence, that any further inquiry would have a reasonable prospect of establishing the truth. Accordingly, examination by a further inquiry could not be said to be warranted," Mr McGinn concluded.

His conclusion came despite the many "disturbing" features and matters of public interest that surrounded Fr Molloy's death.

"Certainly there are extremely unusual, if not unique, features about this case. Many of these are quite disturbing and merited an in-depth analysis. Unfortunately, it appears to me that the precise truth of the events on the 7th and 8th July 1985 cannot now be ascertained," Mr McGinn stated.

The 2015 report put to bed some of the rife speculation and theories that abounded about Fr Molloy's death.

It found no evidence to support claims that Judge Roe was known to the Flynns and Fr Molloy, although such theories have not been wholly disproved.

"It is an uncomfortable fact that the judge at Richard Flynn's trial, Judge Frank Roe, was deeply involved in the horse business, which was something he had in common with Richard and Therese Flynn and with Fr Niall Molloy," the report noted.

"There is no documentary evidence to substantiate the suggestion that the judge was in correspondence with the DPP or to substantiate the suggestion that Judge Roe was predisposed to securing Richard Flynn's acquittal," it added.

Though the Flynns enjoyed friendships with parties involved in politics, the report also found no evidence to support claims that "these political connections were used to their advantage" in relation to the events surrounding Fr Molloy's death.

The report also discounted rumours of a connection between the DPP Eamon Barnes and the Flynn family.

Around the time of Richard's trial, the rumour mill was wild with speculation that Mr Barnes was a sponsor or godfather to one of the Flynn children.

In a statement to senior Gardaí in 2011, Mr Barnes categorically denied the rumours, saying that as far as he was aware he never met any member of the Flynn family.

During the course of their review, Gardaí found no evidence to support claims that the former DPP was acquainted with the Flynns, was godfather to one of their daughters, or attended the Flynn wedding on 6 July 1985.

"The suggestion about being a godfather was investigated by members of the SCRT, who examined the parish records at the church in Tober, Co Offaly, where all four of Richard and Therese Flynn's children had been baptised between 1956 and 1965. The godparents of all four of the children are detailed on these records and Eamonn Barnes is not one of them," the McGinn report stated.

It also detailed sensational and baseless claims contained in anonymous letters to the Molloy family.

One undated letter signed by a 'concerned Midlander who wants justice done' suggested that the priest bled to death following some sort of operation that left the room like a "slaughterhouse" – a claim debunked in the McGinn report and by Gardaí.

The Molloy family also received another letter in July 1986 from someone claiming to be working as a waiter at the wedding function. They claimed to have witnessed an altercation between Richard and Niall downstairs and that he was brought upstairs where a row erupted again. None of the claims made in these letters have been substantiated.

While the McGinn report attempted to draw a line under some of the wilder allegations made about the case over the years, it also underscored the many unanswered questions that remained, such as the exact time of the assault on Fr Molloy and his death.

"Among the questions, which remain unanswered, are the time that Fr Molloy sustained his injuries: the medical evidence suggests that he did not actually die for a considerable period after being injured," the McGinn report found.

Another unexplained fact was the "significant delay in calling the authorities" that night, which had generated considerable speculation and theories over the years to fill the "evidential vacuum", the report noted.

During the SCRT probe, Mr Flynn's only son, David, spoke to Gardaí but was unable to shed any further light on events at Kilcoursey House and insisted that the family did not discuss following "any particular plan of action" on the night.

On this aspect of the case, Mr McGinn concluded: "Much of the conjecture is completely without foundation and some of the theories are actually contradicted by the available evidence. Unfortunately, it appears that the only people who could offer credible evidence in order to explain the delay either have died, are too infirm to speak about it or are unwilling to divulge what occurred."

The report by the senior counsel, however, left the Molloy family with even more unanswered questions, in particular over how Niall's death was investigated in 1985.

Questions over why Gardaí failed to interview guests who attended the Flynn wedding on Saturday, 6 July. Why no door-to-door enquiries were carried out. Why a break-in at Fr Molloy's home in Castlecoote earlier that year was not investigated. Why potential witnesses were not asked to give a statement. Why the veracity of certain key witnesses was not tested. Why Fr Molloy's broken watch was returned to his family without being investigated. Why a key medical report, that could have placed "a different complexion" on the case, was not sought. Why a statement from Fr Molloy's solicitor in relation to a land deal with the Flynns was not included in the investigation.

These were the new set of questions facing the Molloy family who were devastated and "deeply disappointed" with the McGinn report and its conclusion.

In the end, the then Minister for Justice Frances Fitzgerald accepted Mr McGinn's conclusion that a public inquiry was not warranted.

"As Minister for Justice and Equality, I know that it is not always possible to obtain answers for families who have lost a loved one in violent circumstances. The grief felt by families in these circumstances is greatly compounded by not knowing precisely what happened, and not seeing someone unambiguously held to account. I sympathise deeply with Fr Molloy's family and others who have faced this," Minister Fitzgerald said.

When the issue was raised in the Dáil, the then Taoiseach Enda Kenny was dispassionate in his remarks: "Fr Molloy is deceased and nothing we say in this House will bring him back. The Government considered and accepted the McGinn report in the last several weeks, after it was presented to the Minister."

These comments, however, only served to add insult to injury for the Molloy family, who once again felt let down by the State.

Responding to the McGinn report, Henry McCourt said the family had been pushing for answers for more than three decades and it was of little consolation to suggest it was "too late" to get to the truth.

"It's all very well saying that it's too late or that witnesses have passed on because that's what we've been shouting about for a long time. We brought fresh evidence in 1988 when everyone was alive and kicking but nothing was done. It's of no comfort to us to say that it's too late now," Mr McCourt said.

As part of the McGinn review, the senior counsel and legal expert also considered Judge Roe's intervention at the 1986 criminal trial of Richard Flynn.

The trial judge's direction to the jury, to acquit Mr Flynn of the manslaughter and assault of Fr Molloy, was "extraordinary" but was within the law, Mr McGinn found.

Judge Roe had accepted a submission by the defence counsel that the cause of Fr Molloy's death had not been sufficiently proven by the prosecution nor had it been shown that Mr Flynn was not acting in self-defence at the time.

"In light of the confession, made on a number of occasions, by Richard Flynn to inflicting violence on Fr Niall Molloy, the directed acquittal of Richard Flynn at his trial was extraordinary," Mr McGinn concluded in his report.

He added that it was impossible to establish the "exact reasons" behind Judge Roe's decision given that he had since passed away and there was no written ruling of his decision.

"Irrespective of whether or not the trial judge was correct in acting as he did and whatever his motivation was, the state of the law at the time of the trial was such that his decision was not, and is not now, subject to review," Mr McGinn added.

In 1986, the law only allowed the defence to appeal a decision in a criminal trial; the DPP could only lodge an appeal to the Supreme Court in very limited circumstances, mainly on a technical point of law.

In simple terms this meant that the prosecution could not appeal Judge Roe's ruling at the time, something that has since changed.

While the prosecution could not appeal the trial result, the then prosecuting counsel, Raymond Groarke, did raise questions about Judge Roe's ruling in a report to the DPP a month after the trial concluded.

Mr Groarke, who later served as President of the Circuit Court and retired from the bench in 2022, said he disagreed with Judge Roe's decision to acquit on both counts of manslaughter and assault.

In his report, Mr Groarke said he was not surprised that Judge Roe ruled as he did on the manslaughter charge but expressed strong reservations about the judge's decision to acquit on the assault charge.

"The count of assault should not have been withdrawn from the jury. There was ample evidence for the jury to consider whether or not the defence of self-defence was valid," Mr Groarke stated.

From a legal perspective, Mr McGinn concluded that Judge Roe did not make an erroneous ruling but may have misapplied the law: "On any view, Judge Roe did not make a demonstrably wrong ruling on the law. Rather, arguably he misapplied the law in deciding that the evidence in the case was insufficient to be considered by a jury."

He added: "At most, this was a mistake in the assessment of the evidence. Such an assessment was something which could not be corrected or clarified in any meaningful way by the Supreme Court. In any event, even if such an application under Section 34 of the 1967 Act had been made, the law did not permit the verdict to be set aside and, therefore, Richard Flynn's acquittal would have remained unaltered."

In the aftermath of the shock trial result, Judge Roe never ventured an explanation or further commented on the extraordinary intervention that saw Mr Flynn walk free from court.

For Chief Superintendent Christy Mangan, the judge's intervention was significant and played a pivotal role in closing down any examination of further evidence and witnesses in the case.

If Judge Roe had not intervened as he did, it was likely that the business dealings between the Flynns and Fr Molloy would have been called into evidence, as would other members of the Flynn family.

The charge of assault causing harm could have proceeded based on the evidence and admissions of Mr Flynn, according to Chief Superintendent Mangan. "You had a person who had admitted to the assault, so even if you decided that there wasn't enough evidence to convict for manslaughter, surely there was enough evidence to convict for a serious assault," he said.

As a result of Judge Roe's intervention, the trial failed to shed light on the motive for the assault on Fr Molloy, he added.

As highlighted in the McGinn report, the failure to include neuropathology evidence suggesting that Fr Molloy may have survived for several hours before dying represented another significant omission.

"Had this opinion been sought in 1985, a different complexion would have been placed on the accounts given by members of the Flynn family and it can be assumed that more questions would have been asked," the McGinn report stated.

Chief Superintendent Mangan said the failure to include this medical evidence had "a detrimental effect" on the trial.

Having examined samples of Fr Molloy's brain tissue in 1985, neuropathologist Dr Michael Farrell believed that the priest had lived for between three and six hours after being assaulted.

His assessment informed the State Pathologist Dr John Harbison's conclusion that the cause of death was due to head injuries but, critically, it was not sought by Gardaí or included in the Book of Evidence.

"I think it would have directed the investigation in a completely different direction," Superintendent Mangan said.

If this "very strong" medical evidence was presented in court, he said, it would have presented a difficulty for Judge Roe in acquitting Mr Flynn.

"That would have indicated that he lay there and he didn't receive medical intervention and that to me is critical. How can you leave somebody lying there, literally dying," the senior investigator said, adding that this medical evidence would have prompted questions over the actions or inactions of those present at the scene on the night.

Further unavoidable questions over several shortcomings in the original Garda investigation, as identified by the SCRT, have lingered since the publication of the McGinn findings.

In addition to the series of omissions identified in the 1985 investigation, the forensic examination of samples from the crime scene and parties involved was found to be incomplete.

The SCRT was also unable to access key exhibits and evidence from the original investigation, something which Chief Superintendent Christopher Mangan found to be completely unsatisfactory. "The fact that the exhibits pertaining to the case were not available was grossly unacceptable," he said.

But one of the more fundamental shortcomings was the failure by Gardaí to include a statement from Fr Molloy's solicitor in relation to the 1984 land deal with the Flynns, described in the McGinn report as a "significant omission".

There was no statement on file from the Athlone-based solicitor, who acted for Fr Molloy and Mrs Flynn, despite the fact that he had been visited by two Garda Detectives within days of the priest's death.

The solicitor was interviewed in relation to the alleged financial difficulties between the parties, something that was alluded to in the Book of Evidence but which lacked this vital statement in support. He was, however, considered as a witness by the Attorney General's Office at Niall's inquest.

Three decades later, these shortcomings in the Garda investigation, in addition to the failure to include Dr Farrell's crucial medical evidence, reignited the sense of loss, anger and injustice for the Molloy family.

"I felt the way I did at Niall's funeral in 1985; it was just like a bereavement all over again," Bill Maher said.

"The McGinn report and the Serious Crime Review Team identified numerous breaches of procedures in the original investigation, where many basic enquiries or checks were not carried out," he added.

The findings confirmed concerns long-held by the Molloy family that the original Garda investigation was "botched" and "shambolic at best".

"The report raises even more questions and confirms our worst fears in relation to the initial Garda investigation. Questions are still there and are even louder now. I believe very strongly that the many shortcomings in the initial Garda investigation alone warrant a Commission of Investigation," Henry McCourt explained.

"The report leaves an awful lot of unanswered questions and compounds the sense of injustice felt by the family. It shows the complete and utter failure of the system, wilfully or otherwise," he added.

In the aftermath of the McGinn report, the then Justice Minister and Tánaiste Frances Fitzgerald acknowledged the "deficiencies" identified in the original investigation but reiterated her belief that an inquiry was unlikely to provide answers.

In a letter to the Molloy family, Minister Fitzgerald said: "These deficiencies were acknowledged in both the work of the SCRT, and also in Mr McGinn's analysis. While some of the issues identified reflect the way in which crime investigation has evolved and become more sophisticated over time, these deficiencies are nevertheless certainly a matter of regret."

Meanwhile, comments by the then Garda Commissioner Noirin O'Sullivan, who said the McGinn report would bring some comfort to the Molloy family, did little to help.

The remark irked Fr Molloy's relatives, who sought clarification on the shortcomings identified in the 1985 Garda investigation.

The Garda Commissioner declined to comment further on the matter but a spokesperson subsequently confirmed that the McGinn report would be examined to see what lessons could be learnt.

The Molloy family, however, remained unconvinced and proceeded to make a complaint about the substandard investigation to the Garda Siochána Ombudsman Commission (GSOC) in 2016. This was their second attempt to have GSOC look into the case.

Their complaint centred on the investigation shortcomings and the loss of potentially vital exhibits and materials gathered as part of the 1985 investigation, such as original crime scene exhibits and handwritten statements, which the SCRT were unable to locate.

The "unprofessional" and "unacceptable" 1985 Garda investigation led to a "serious miscarriage of justice" in the case, the family submitted.

In the end, the limited powers available to GSOC, who cannot compel retired members of the force to engage, precluded it from fully examining the complaint.

In July 2018, GSOC published a report excoriating the Garda handling of vital evidence and exhibits in a crime that remained open and unsolved but which potentially could have benefited from advances in forensics.

"While individuals and their actions, or failures to act, in 1985 and 1986 cannot be investigated further, it is of real concern to

GSOC that exhibits and documents relevant to the case can now not be found," GSOC said in a statement.

In advance of the report being published, GSOC Chair, former judge Mary Ellen Ring, wrote to the Acting Garda Commissioner to register GSOC's ongoing concern over the loss of evidential materials and exhibits in the Molloy case and others.

"Safekeeping of documents and exhibits has become even more pertinent with the developments we see on a regular basis in relation to forensic advances and the ability to solve serious cases years, and decades later, continues to develop apace. Thus this knowledge places an even higher onus on police services to keep safe the documents and evidence which could make a prosecution successful into the future, even where witnesses may have moved on or died," the GSOC Chair said.

"In this case we have relatives of the late Father Molloy who have lost a loved family member and where the circumstances of that death thirty years later still causes pain. This pain sadly has been compounded by a belief that a poor investigation was carried out into their uncle's death at the time. The lack of regard shown to the evidence and documentation in this matter in the intervening years by Gardaí in many ways adds insult to injury which is clearly not a result anyone would wish to see," the former judge added.

The Commission sought a progress report from Gardaí on plans for a new Property and Exhibit Management System (PEMS).

It also pointed out that the safekeeping of exhibits had already been flagged as an issue in a 2014 Garda Inspectorate report, which stated: "During field visits, Gardaí were asked where case files are kept and the consistent response was 'everywhere'. The majority of Gardaí stated that files are kept in their lockers. In extreme cases, locations for keeping files included members taking them home. The retention of files by individual Gardaí removes the ability of supervisors to check the progression of cases and if officers are away from work for extended periods, then files are not readily available."

GSOC subsequently received a response from the Garda Commissioner's office setting out key changes in how exhibits are managed to mitigate against any materials being misplaced or lost into the future.

In 2019, Garda HQ published a new policy and protocol for managing property and exhibits and PEMS training was later rolled out. In 2021, around 27 staff members were recorded as PEMS officers across the country.

The response to the GSOC complaint, however, brought little comfort for the Molloy family, who once again called on the Justice Minister to mount a Commission of Investigation.

"It simply goes to the very root of our justice system and I would submit it is something which must be done to alleviate the unease and unrest surrounding this case for the past 33 years, not just for the benefit of the family members but also for the benefit of members of the public and parishioners of my late uncle, who to this day are disgusted and upset with the findings as above outlined in relation to this case together with the inability to bring the matter to a satisfactory conclusion to date," Henry McCourt wrote in a letter to the Justice Minister.

The comments reflect the Molloy family's deep and growing frustration over the State's handling of Niall's death over a period of more than three decades.

Over the past decade alone, the family have made repeated calls for a Commission of Investigation but have been rejected at every turn, despite the glaring deficiencies in how the case was handled.

In his report, Mr McGinn said there was an understandable quest for justice when a life is prematurely cut short by a human act.

In the Molloy case, however, Mr McGinn found that this had not happened: "Following the death of Fr Niall Molloy, such a quest has been frustrated by a number of different factors, all of which have accumulated to give rise to a completely reasonable sense of injustice."

All dressed up Niall was the youngest of nine children born to Senator William J. Molloy. In this photo from 1938/1939, he is playing dress-up with his sisters

Trophy winner Niall was an accomplished horseman from an early age, winning a show jumping event at the Claremorris Show when he was just 14 years old

Family home Carrowroe House, on the outskirts of Roscommon town, where Niall and his siblings grew up

Army mission Niall served as an Army Chaplain in the Defence forces and spent seven months in Cyprus as part of a UN peacekeeping mission with the 23rd Infantry Group in 1972

In training Niall studied at the Irish College in Rome before being ordained a priest in 1957
(Image: Sean Browne)

Important occasion Fr Molloy was chief celebrant at the 55th anniversary event of the 1916 Rising in Arbour Hill, where President Eamon de Valera (to his right) attended. It was De Valera who had stood Senator Molloy up in New York decades earlier. Partially obscured by Taoiseach Jack Lynch (on the left, behind Fr Molloy) was Brian Lenihan, who attended the wedding in Kilcoursey in 1985 *(Image: Irish Photo Archive)*

Unsolved mystery Fr Molloy pictured in happier times

Death scene Niall was found dead in the master bedroom of Kilcoursey House outside Clara in Offaly, the home of Richard and Therese Flynn. He was a frequent caller to the house and had his own bedroom there *(Image: Derek Speirs)*

Under scrutiny Richard and Therese Flynn photographed following the inquest into Niall's death in July 1986 *(Image: Derek Speirs)*

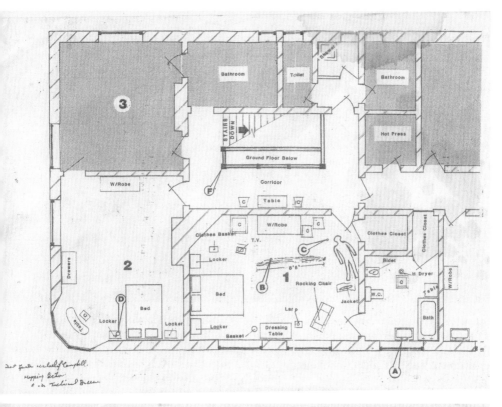

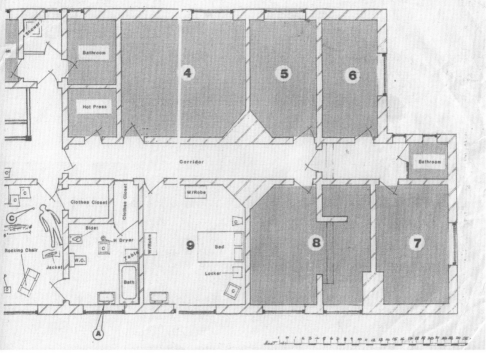

Inside the house Drawings showing the master bedroom where Fr Molloy was found dead, as well as the layout of adjacent rooms and the stair landing at Kilcoursey House. Room 2 was known as Niall's room, but Room 9 was entered in evidence as his room by the Gardaí

Stepping in Judge Thomas Frank Roe made an extraordinary intervention at Richard Flynn's trial, directing the jury to acquit him of all charges after a doubt was raised in the medical evidence *(Image: Derek Speirs)*

Quest for justice Niall's brother, Billy Molloy, and his nephew, Ian Maher, pressed for answers after the conflicting trial and inquest outcomes and pushed for the case to be reopened, to no avail *(Image: John Carlos)*

Witness Kilbeggan GP Dr Daniel O'Sullivan, who pronounced Fr Molloy dead at the scene, told Niall's inquest that Richard Flynn informed him of a row downstairs that night *(Image: Derek Speirs)*

Media spotlight Fr Molloy's death made headlines at home and abroad. Journalist Gene Kerrigan was among many reporters to write about the case, as this front cover of current affairs magazine, Magill, shows

(Image: Derek Speirs)

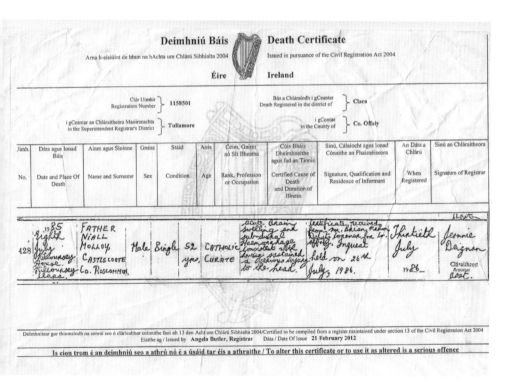

Death certificate Fr Molloy's death certificate shows that he died of acute brain swelling and subdural haemorrhage as a result of an injury to the head

Kind soul The last known photo of Niall, taken on 6 July 1985. This photo hangs in every house in Castlecoote parish

Chapter 9
THE LAND DEAL

It was a shared passion for horses that led to Fr Niall Molloy and Therese Flynn forging a business partnership from the 1970s onwards.

Over the course of this largely informal joint venture, tens of thousands of pounds passed through Therese and Niall's joint Allied Irish Bank account, just one of several bank accounts they used.

As part of the more recent review of the Molloy case, Gardaí were able to verify elements of the business relationship between the priest and the Flynns but not to the extent that would have been possible in the 1980s.

Several witnesses confirmed to Gardaí that Niall and Therese jointly traded in property, horses and cattle over the years.

One witness, whose husband had in the past managed horses for Therese and Fr Molloy, confirmed that the pair paid their bills to the riding centre by cheques drawn on a joint account.

The holding of a joint bank account was corroborated by other witnesses.

Another witness, a local farmer, who occasionally carried out work at Kilcoursey House told Gardaí that Niall was there every second day and he believed that the priest was the "paymaster".

Other witnesses, who had worked at Kilcoursey, however, maintained that they were always paid by Richard or Therese Flynn rather than Fr Molloy.

As part of the research carried out for the recent documentary, however, a trawl of available records provided some insight into the joint business interests of Fr Molloy and Mrs Flynn.

The lifelong friends jointly owned farm land in Moydrum, north of Athlone town, some of which was sold to a local gun club in 1982.

In the early 1980s they also unsuccessfully sought outline planning permission to build three houses on the Moydrum holding. The planning application for the houses was only in Therese's name, as were most of the horse trading transactions.

There was nothing out of the ordinary about these dealings.

In 1984, documents show that the Flynns and Fr Molloy were in the process of purchasing a house and smallholding in the heart of Connemara in County Galway that summer.

The parties intended to purchase a house at Derryinver, near Letterfrack, for IR£22,000, although the purpose or intended use of the property remains uncertain.

The holding extended to less than an acre and would not have provided much ground to accommodate horses so maybe it was intended to serve as a holiday home for the long-standing friends.

The sale, however, was stymied in September when it emerged that there was a problem with the property's planning permission. Records held by Galway County Council suggest there was an unauthorised development on the site.

On 5 September 1984, documents relating to the proposed sale detail a phone message from Fr Molloy in relation to the

Derryinver planning permission being "wrong" and the sale not going ahead.

Within hours, a new plan of action was made. A memo from Fr Molloy's solicitor, dated 5 September, notes a plan to buy land from Mr Flynn at Kilcoursey with the price to be agreed.

This unusual agreement, for Therese to buy land from Richard that she presumably already owned, was drafted when the Flynn businesses were in trouble and needed a cash injection.

Over the next two days, Fr Molloy and Mr and Mrs Flynn visited their solicitor's office in Athlone to finalise the terms of the new agreement.

It was originally drafted for IR£50,000 for 40 acres of land at Kilcoursey House but this was amended to IR£35,000 for 38 acres, with an unusually large deposit of IR£24,000.

The deal was signed on 7 September 1984, with the deposit to be split between Fr Molloy and Mrs Flynn. It is understood that the funds were deposited with Richard Flynn directly and not held in the solicitor's client account.

Documents also show that in November 1984, the priest updated his legal firm about the land deal and an amended folio map. "Everything is alright now. I know you will push forward with all haste," he wrote.

The next step was to seek approval for the Kilcoursey deal from the Land Commission, an arm of the Department of Agriculture, and an application was submitted before the year ended.

In February 1985, however, the Commission ruled the proposed Kilcoursey deal out of contention on the basis that it would create two 'uneconomic holdings' of land.

That same month, documents further reveal that Niall and Therese also sold a parcel of land in Moydrum for IR£14,000.

The timing of these transactions is key, occurring just months prior to Fr Molloy's death. Their significance, however, did not come to light until after the priest was found dead at Kilcoursey House later that summer.

It was only then that Niall's solicitor shared some insights into the business partnership with the Molloy family and told of the priest's anxiety over the failed land deal and monies owing.

The solicitor, who acted for Niall and Therese since 1972, advised Niall's sister, Suzanna and her daughter, also Susanna, that the Flynn businesses were in difficulty and cash was needed in a hurry when the deal was made.

Niall, he added, had reservations about the land deal but Therese had reassured him that if anything went wrong the deposit would be returned.

The Athlone-based solicitor also confirmed that in the wake of the collapsed deal, Niall had tried to recover his share of the deposit but without success.

He also told them that Therese had asked him whether he was obliged to inform the Molloy family of the failed land deal, after Niall's death.

Despite subsequent claims by the Flynns that the deposit was repaid to Fr Molloy, there is no documentary evidence of the large sum of monies being returned to the priest prior to his death and none was proffered by the Flynns in 1985.

When Gardaí became aware of the financial transaction just days after Niall's death, they sought clarity on the land deal as part of their investigation.

On two occasions, Richard Flynn declined to be interviewed or make a statement to Gardaí about the matter.

Instead, Therese agreed to speak to Gardaí in the presence of her solicitor.

In her interview, Therese insisted that she had repaid IR£11,000 in cash from a safe to Niall around two months before his death, although she accepted that she could not provide a receipt or proof of payment.

She also told Gardaí that it had been Fr Molloy's idea to purchase the land because he had wanted to retire and build a house at Kilcoursey.

Mr Lysaght confirmed to Gardaí that no documents or records were available as proof that the deposit was repaid. He also committed to provide Gardaí with a further statement from Therese on the land and financial transactions but no such statement is evident or features in the Book of Evidence.

Today, there is still a question mark over how much Fr Molloy actually paid over to the Flynns in 1984, as well as whether any monies were repaid after the deal fell asunder.

As part of the recent investigation into the priest's death, Garda were unable to verify the sum paid over by Fr Molloy and, given the financial difficulties facing the Flynns at the time, suspect that he may have paid over the entire deposit of IR£24,000 to Richard.

Gardaí also found no documentary evidence to corroborate Therese's assertion that the deposit was repaid. Casting further doubt over the claim, Chief Superintendent Christopher Mangan told the Molloy family there was no evidence that a safe existed at Kilcoursey House.

###

A key unanswered question in the mystery surrounding Fr Molloy's violent death is one of motive.

Even when Gardaí first investigated the suspicious death, they were unsure of the real reason behind the violence that ultimately killed the gentle-natured cleric.

In the absence of any explanation, backed up by evidence, Gardaí could only speculate as to motive. They considered Richard Flynn's version of events that a "silly row" erupted over drink, they acknowledged Billy Molloy's assertion that Mr Flynn had told him of a political row that night and they also considered that money may have been a factor in the events that led to Niall's death.

Having spoken to members of the Molloy family, Gardaí were aware that Richard owed Niall a "substantial sum of money" in 1985 in relation to a land deal that failed to go ahead.

Despite this knowledge, the business dealings between Fr Molloy and the Flynns were not pursued or examined in any great detail by Gardaí at the time.

More significantly, any opportunities to raise the financial dealings at the criminal trial of Mr Flynn were thwarted by Judge Frank Roe's intervention to cut proceedings short.

The paper trail then and now, however, lends some support to the theory that money may have been at the heart of the row that unfolded on that summer Sunday night.

As revealed here and in the recent documentary, there was a sense of urgency around some of the land deals and transactions pursued by the Flynns and Fr Molloy in the months before his death.

In more recent years, David Flynn, Richard and Therese's only son, acknowledged that the family did face financial difficulties in 1985 when he spoke to the SCRT in 2011 and 2012.

Speaking to Gardaí on a voluntary basis, Mr Flynn described the family businesses as being "asset rich but cash poor" at the time.

He also pointed out that while times were tough in the 1980s, his father had managed to keep various businesses afloat without the need to lay off any staff.

The relationship between Fr Molloy and his parents, he maintained, was good at the time of the July wedding.

He also commented that his mother and Niall had a bond that was in many ways "stronger than any husband-wife relationship".

In addition to concerns over the failed land deal and monies owing, several witnesses also told Gardaí, during the original investigation and in the more recent probe, of Fr Molloy's intention to sever his business ties with the Flynns prior to his death.

One of those witnesses was Martin Molloy, a cousin of Niall's, who had frequently purchased livestock and horses on his behalf.

Just weeks before the Flynn wedding, Mr Molloy had spoken to Niall and arranged to buy a dozen cattle, which was paid out of the joint business account.

At the time, Fr Molloy had a black eye but he declined to elaborate or give further details to his cousin of what had happened.

Niall had also confided in him that he planned to dissolve the business partnership with Therese.

The priest said he was getting out of horses and hoped to sell two that were being stabled in Clara before leaving on a long holiday to America.

As part of the recent TV documentary, Chief Superintendent Christopher Mangan confirmed that Fr Molloy had wished to end his business partnership with the Flynns.

"From my enquiries, it would appear that Fr Niall Molloy wanted to disentangle himself from his business dealings at that time. He wanted to move on. There was information that he intended travelling abroad and also that he needed a plot of land to build a house and retire and that would appear to be the situation," he told the production team.

The Garda investigation considered what assets may have been jointly owned by Niall and Therese but was unable to establish a clear picture.

The Molloy family believed the assets involved horses and cattle and may even have included valuable artworks by Jack B Yeats.

"What we found was that there were some cattle bought, some horses bought, but there were some very valuable paintings that could never be accounted for. And if they existed, we were never able to recover them for the estate of Fr Niall Molloy," Chief Superintendent Mangan said.

In another twist, some curious and unusual evidence also emerged during the making of the documentary that added to the intrigue surrounding Niall and Therese's relationship.

There was never any evidence of any romantic connection between the long-time friends but, strangely, two documents suggesting that Therese was Niall's sibling were uncovered.

The first revelation came in 1988, when it emerged that Therese had allegedly tried to cash in on a life insurance policy in Niall's name, which named her as his sister. It was around this time too that the Molloy family pushed for the case to be reopened in light of new medical evidence.

In addition to this insurance claim, the documentary team uncovered another document relating to the proposed Connemara property deal in 1984 which also detailed the businesswoman as Niall's sister.

29th June, 1984.

Attendance on Fr. Molloy, Castlecoote, Roscommon.

You phoned me today in connection with a small house on a quarter of an acre near Renvyle, Connemara which you and your sister Mrs. Flynn are purchasing for £22,000. The Auctioneers are Keane, Mahony Smith, Galway and you are paying them a Booking Deposit of £1,000 and asking them to get the Vendor's Solicitors to send us a Contract etc.

N/F.

Although the author of the 'memo of attendance for Fr Molloy' is unclear, the note was dated in June 1984 when plans were being drafted to purchase the house near Letterfrack.

"You phoned me today in connection with a small house on a quarter of an acre near Renvyle, Connemara which you and your sister Mrs Flynn are purchasing for £22,000," it read.

Yet again, this amounted to potentially critical information that could have altered the direction of the first Garda investigation.

More than three decades on, it seems incredible that the financial dealings between Fr Molloy and the Flynns were never fully explored or pursued as part of the original Garda investigation or during Richard's trial. The 2015 McGinn report acknowledged that the failure of the Flynns to be upfront about the land deal with Fr Molloy was "suspicious" but warned against drawing any concrete conclusions from this fact.

"It is suspicious that the business dealings which were ongoing between the Flynns and Fr Molloy were not revealed to the authorities at the outset of the Garda investigation and only came to light subsequently," the report concluded.

"Certainly the most obvious inference to draw from this would be that Richard and Therese Flynn did not wish this to be revealed because it indicated that a financial advantage might have been accrued to them following Fr Molloy's death," it added.

Today, the Molloy family remain extremely aggrieved over the failure to fully investigate the failed land deal and business dealings, as well as suggestions that Therese was a sister of Fr Niall.

"The whole area of the business was never given focus and should have been from the first week of his death. It was glossed over for whatever reason. Carelessness, negligence, deliberately? I don't know," Henry McCourt said.

Chapter 10
THE FLYNN FINANCES

In 1985, Richard and Therese Flynn appeared to have it all. They ran several businesses, were planning a holiday in France that summer, and were looking forward to laying on a lavish wedding for their eldest daughter, Maureen, at the family homestead, a plush 23-roomed mansion.

With connections in business and political circles, by 1980s standards the Flynns were considered well-off.

Richard owned and ran a chain of motor accessory shops across the country while his wife, Therese, ran the family-owned coffee shop in Athlone and also pursued her interest in horses with Fr Niall Molloy.

Unfortunately, it has not been possible for the Molloy family to build a complete or clear picture of Niall's business dealings with the Flynns, with many records lost or unavailable over the years.

There is evidence, however, that the Flynn finances were on the wane from 1983 onwards, as revealed in the recent TV documentary.

This lends some weight to the possibility that the Molloy-Flynn business partnership may have been in trouble at the time and raises the question – was the Flynns' apparent affluence merely a façade?

###

Richard Flynn was not afraid to try new things. He came from farming stock and ran a large cattle farm in Tober, Offaly, up until the late 1970s when an outbreak of brucellosis prompted him to change direction.

Around 1978, Richard purchased Kilcoursey House, just outside Clara, and left the farming life behind to instead try his hand at the retail and service sector – selling coffees and car accessories.

It was not his first attempt to go into business. A decade earlier, he had sought planning permission to develop a petrol station outside Moate on the main route between Dublin and Galway.

When the application was refused in November 1968, Richard sought support from the then Education Minister, Brian Lenihan Senior, a local politician and family friend.

In a letter to Westmeath County Council in May 1969, the Fianna Fáil Minister wrote: "I wish to make representations on behalf of Mr Richard Flynn, Moate, Co Westmeath, who has applied to your council for planning permission to erect a filling station at Ardnapondra, Moate. I would be glad if you would let me know the position in this matter at your earliest convenience."

It was not unusual at that time for politicians to lend their support for such local business ventures. The intervention, however, failed to win over the council, which refused the application on appeal later that year, citing road safety concerns.

Richard set his sights on opening a chain of shops selling car accessories, such as seat covers, lights, bumpers and all things car-related.

The shops were branded Richspeed and grew in number over time, with outlets in Dublin, Limerick, Galway, Ennis and Sligo, as well as in the midlands.

While Richard and his son, David, were managing the Richspeed chain of businesses into the 1980s, the Flynns also owned a coffee shop in Athlone Shopping Centre, run by Therese.

As already stated, Mrs Flynn was trading in horses, cattle and land with Niall for more than a decade.

By 1985, Richard and Therese were registered as directors of Athlone Coffee Shop Ltd, Richspeed Auto Accessories Ltd and RKF Motor Factors Ltd; Richard was also a registered director for K&R Development Ltd. David Flynn was appointed a director of Richspeed Auto Accessories Ltd and RKF Motor Factors Ltd in May 1985.

Outwardly, the Flynn finances and business empire appeared to be thriving. The available paper trail, however, would suggest that the cracks were beginning to show in the early 1980s.

While it is not possible to build a complete picture of all of the Flynn companies, the annual returns filed for Richspeed Auto Accessories provide some insight into the changing fortunes facing the family.

Between 1978 and 1982 the annual returns for Richspeed Auto Accessories looked healthy, with no debts registered against the company.

That all changed, however, in December 1983 when Bank of Ireland registered two charges against Richspeed Auto Accessories in respect of a mortgage on a retail unit at the Northside Shopping

Centre in Dublin and a unit at Athlone Shopping Centre. The 1983 annual return filed with the Companies Registration Office (CRO) further shows that Richspeed Auto Accessories had debts amounting to IR£23,110 at the time.

Under the Companies Act 1963, businesses were required to register outstanding mortgage debts and charges with the CRO.

The level of indebtedness facing the company, however, did not feature on official CRO records at that time as the 1983 annual return was not filed until 1987.

Within months, there were further signs that the Flynn finances may have been in difficulty.

In July 1984, a year before Fr Molloy's death, the family solicitor wrote to the Land Commission on Richard's behalf seeking compensation and threatening legal action for alleged losses arising from a compulsory purchase order completed seven years earlier.

The legal letter, from the National Archives, claimed that Mr Flynn had suffered "substantial loss and damage" as a result of the 1977 compulsory purchase of lands at Tober in Offaly, where he had previously lived and farmed.

He retained what had been the family home, Tober House, for his son, David, and moved to Kilcoursey House, a few miles away.

It is not clear if any legal action followed but the letter to the Land Commission and Attorney General demanding compensation may provide a hint of some financial difficulties beginning to emerge for Mr Flynn and his businesses.

Later that year, the Athlone coffee shop run by the Flynns also featured in a court report in the local press. In November, Richard was named as a defendant in a civil action taken against three tenants of Athlone Shopping Centre for alleged unpaid service charges. The case was struck out, however, as the presiding judge refused to accept photocopied documents presented in court.

By the close of 1984, Richspeed Autos had registered debts of more than IR£24,000.

Critically, as detailed in the previous chapter, this was when plans were hastily drawn up for Therese and Niall to purchase lands from Richard for the sum of IR£35,000, after the Letterfrack sale fell through that summer.

The considerable sums of money beg the question – was the Kilcoursey land deal deposit of IR£24,000 agreed to bridge this financial hole in the Flynn finances?

Meanwhile, the financial position at Richspeed Autos was continuing to decline, with the level of debt racking up year on year.

A year after Fr Niall's death and shortly after Richard Flynn's truncated trial, legal representatives for the Flynns sought clarification on what land assets may have been jointly owned between Therese and her business partner of many years.

A month later, just days after the inquest verdict, a further legal letter to Niall and Therese's solicitor in Athlone claimed that any property was "in fact and in law" belonging to Mrs Flynn.

Shortly afterwards, her husband opened a new Richspeed shop at the Crescent Shopping Centre in Limerick. The new store was opened after a Richspeed Autos unit closed in the upmarket Blackrock Shopping Centre in Dublin the previous Christmas following an alleged row over rents owing, according to press reports.

On the face of it, it was a mixed picture for the Flynn businesses at a time when the economic recession was biting hard.

The official picture at the time was less than clear, as company records were not filed with the CRO until 1987, two years after Niall's death.

Those late annual returns show that the level of indebtedness at Richspeed Autos grew from IR£23,110 in 1983 to IR£32,794 by 1985, and rose rapidly to IR£115,311 by 1986.

In late 1986, Barclays Bank also registered a floating charge against Richspeed Autos against all company assets, both present or future.

A year later a separate charge was registered against the company for monies owed on properties in Sligo, Galway, Ennis and Limerick.

The records filed for the other Flynn businesses are thin on detail and fail to shed any light on the financial position of these companies in the early 1980s.

The returns for Richspeed Autos, though, do point to growing mortgage debts registered by Bank of Ireland and Barclays Bank.

Within a relatively short period following Niall's death, the Flynn financial woes continued to stack up, forcing the family to consider offloading assets.

In August 1987, Fr Molloy's estate mounted civil proceedings against Richard for funeral and legal expenses and special damages for the priest's death.

Meanwhile, Therese mounted a countersuit against the priest's estate for IR£6,000 relating to a horse. It was claimed that Niall had lodged the monies following the sale of a horse just weeks before his death to his personal account rather than the joint account held by the business partners – the legal action was later dropped.

By September 1987, the Flynns were forced to put Kilcoursey House on the market to meet significant debts registered by

Barclays Bank and the Revenue Commissioners, which together ran into hundreds of thousands of pounds.

The period residence on 60 acres was expected to fetch in the region of IR£250,000-£300,000 when it was listed for auction in October that year.

National press reports outlined in great detail the prominence of the substantial property, which included a stable yard, a sand ring for breaking horses, two grass tennis courts, a walled orchard and kitchen garden, as well as a two-bedroomed gate lodge. Such was the status of the sale, the property was even advertised in the *Wall Street Journal*.

The adverts barely alluded to the death of a priest two years previously, with one newspaper merely noting that Kilcoursey House was the "subject of much media attention some time ago".

Given the high-profile nature of Fr Molloys death and subsequent trial and inquest, however, it was almost impossible not to know of its provenance.

When Kilcoursey House opened its doors to prospective buyers, there was considerable interest, although viewing was by appointment only and several people were turned away at the door.

Locally, some believed Kilcoursey House would be hard to sell. "I don't know if they'll be able to sell the house. Who'd buy a house that a priest was killed in or that anybody was killed in?" one local man told a Sunday newspaper. "Nobody's going to buy that house and sleep in a room where a priest lay dead on the floor," another said.

The auction was scheduled for 3pm on 29 October 1987 in the offices of Gunne Auctioneers, Ballsbridge. The asking price was IR£250,000.

On 23 October 1987 Ian Maher lodged a High Court action, a Lis Pendens, against Kilcoursey House for the IR£11,000 he suspected was never repaid to Fr Niall from the doomed Kilcoursey land deal.

The auction could not go ahead with such a legal action pending.

There had been no record of the amount being paid back in the form of either a receipt, or a lodgement to Niall's bank.

In response to the action, Therese claimed that IR£7,200 or IR£8,200 was paid to Niall within a few weeks of the Land Commission's refusal of permission to purchase the land from Richard. This had taken place around March 1985 and she had paid the monies in cash from a safe in the house, she claimed. She said she cleared the balance in May 1985 but offered to pay the Molloys an additional IR£12,000 once the sale of Kilcoursey was completed.

Ian refused the offer and held strong.

The move saw Kilcoursey House being withdrawn from auction at the last minute. It meant that the deeds of the property would now put prospective buyers on notice that legal action was pending.

In light of the High Court action, efforts to sell Kilcoursey House changed – instead of auction, the property was now being offered for sale by tender.

Around the same time, the Revenue Commissioners secured High Court judgements against Mr Flynn for over IR£126,000 in taxes owed on the Athlone coffee shop and the Richspeed businesses.

By March 1988, the coffee shop unit in Athlone Shopping Centre had ceased trading and was put up for auction. The last annual return filed for the business was in 1986.

As the Flynn businesses continued to crumble and the debts stacked up, the family was unable to secure a buyer for Kilcoursey House.

In April 1988, Fr Molloy's estate was awarded a settlement of IR£13,141 in damages when the civil action came to court.

That same year, both Richard and Therese resigned as directors from Richspeed Autos. The company was subsequently taken over but ultimately folded.

A second attempt to sell Kilcoursey House at auction in June 1991 failed when it was withdrawn at IR£200,000 but it was reportedly purchased privately later that year.

When the sale went through, the outstanding settlement was finally made to the Molloy family.

In the wake of Niall's death, his family made several attempts to establish the full extent of jointly owned assets. Despite repeated requests for documents or records, the Molloy family were denied access and stonewalled at every turn.

The Flynn family solicitor, Liam Lysaght, previously acted on Niall and Therese's behalf but denied representing the priest at any stage. The family took the matter up with the Law Society. In 1993, he was censured by the Society and by a Judge of the High Court and ordered to pay a fine of IR£500.

Chapter 11
THE INSURANCE POLICY AND WILL

Within weeks of Fr Niall Molloy's death in July 1985, an unusual claim was made on a life insurance policy in his name. The claim on Accident Policy No. 9257985 was made to the Combined Insurance Company on 5 August 1985. The policy had been taken out on 30 November 1984.

The documentation suggested that the claim came from the main beneficiary, Fr Molloy's 'sister', Therese Flynn. A handwritten note signed by a 'Therese Flynn' stated that Niall was dead and she wanted the necessary forms to make a claim.

When the insurers requested his death certificate and Letters of Administration, they heard nothing more from the claimant.

The Molloy family only discovered the policy and the alleged attempt to cash in on it in 1988, after they were awarded over IR£13,000 in an action against Richard Flynn for damages arising from Niall's death.

There had been no record of the policy in Fr Molloy's papers and no evidence from the bank statements they could locate that he paid a premium.

When it came to public attention in April 1988, Therese claimed she had not written the note to the insurance company and a handwriting expert was called upon to confirm if it was her signature on the note. He said it was not, but the Molloy family had their doubts, and they thought Niall's signature looked different to his usual one.

In the end, having proven that Therese was no relation whatsoever, the Molloys were paid out on the policy, to the tune of about IR£1,100.

This all happened at a time when the Molloy family had secured fresh medical evidence that Fr Molloy had survived for hours on the night he died.

Combined with the revelation about the insurance policy and the claim that Therese was Niall's sister, the Molloys requested the case be reopened. However, despite engaging with senior detectives in An Garda Siochána, it was not to be.

There were also questions over Niall's will and testament, a copy of which the Molloy family have not been able to locate over the past three decades.

Billy Molloy, the priest's brother and the administrator of his estate, took out probate on 13 June 1986, the day after Richard Flynn's trial concluded. The amount in Fr Molloy's estate that could be found at that time was IR£6,278.15.

The Flynns also showed an interest in locating Fr Molloy's will. After Richard's trial, their solicitor, Liam Lysaght wrote to the Department of Defence on 7 July 1986, as follows: "Our client believes that the late Fr Niall Molloy made a will while a member of the Defence Forces. Our client was informed by Fr Molloy that he had made this will before leaving for Cyprus and that the will contained directions to our client."

On the same date, the Flynn solicitor wrote to Niall and Therese's solicitor in Athlone about the business partnership. "Mrs Flynn has consulted me for advice as to the legal ownership of certain assets which apparently the late Fr Molloy's family will claim form part of his estate," the letter outlined, adding that the only business dealings of concern were the purchase and sale of Moydrum farm and the proposed purchase of land at Kilcoursey.

Meanwhile, the Department of Defence was also being asked about the priest's will, which had been raised as a Parliamentary Question on the floor of the Dáil.

No will was on record as being deposited with the Army, but there was a note dated 26 September 1972, shortly before Niall departed for Cyprus, from the Officer of Records to the Head Chaplain.

The note confirmed that Fr Molloy, who was due to travel to Cyprus with the 23rd Infantry Squad, had deposited a will with a colleague in the diocese: "Fr Molloy informs me that his will is held by (a priest), St. Mary's, Sligo."

There was also an undated will template on file, issued by the Army, but with scant information. It named two executors, a vet in Tullamore and a doctor in Sligo. It also named the priest in St. Mary's in Sligo as the person in receipt of Niall's will, but there was no date or signature on this document, or any details of assets, beneficiaries or wishes.

On 9 July 1986, the Department of Defence informed the Flynn's family solicitor that the will was made and deposited with the Elphin Diocese in Sligo. The response was cleared by the Chief State Solicitor, according to a note on file.

Available documents suggest that the Department of Defence was concerned about how to respond to the requests from legal

THE INSURANCE POLICY AND WILL

representatives for the Molloys and the Flynns and given the publicity surrounding his will.

In a memo dated 1 August 1986, the Department noted: "In view of the press and publicity given to the topic of the late Fr Molloy's will, I consulted the Chief State Solicitor, Mr Louis Dockery. In his opinion there is no legal obligation on the Department to take an initiative regards disclosure of information but he does feel that there is a strong social obligation. He advised that the Department should make the same information available to Messrs Claffey Gannon and Co. (Billy Molloy's solicitor) as had been given to Mr Lysaght."

On 5 August 1986, Mr Lysaght followed up on his letter to the Athlone solicitor, writing: "From all the information presently available, it appears to me that all of the property dealt with by Mrs Flynn and the late Fr Molloy together was property, in fact and in law, belonging to Mrs Flynn. There is a growing body of evidence that the late Fr Molloy left a will. I am making further enquiries in this regard and, subject to your kind approval, I propose contacting you on my return from holidays at the beginning of September."

As it transpired, the sizeable property at Moydrum was under a tenant in common arrangement, meaning if one partner died, the other did not assume their share or ownership.

The Chief State Solicitor subsequently wrote to the Department of Defence on 23 September 1986 to say that no information was available but that if further details came to hand about the will "it would be proper to pass on to the solicitors".

Then in November in response to a Parliamentary Question about Niall's will, the Department outlined its position on the now contentious matter.

In a letter dated 14 November 1986, Lieutenant Colonel MF Minihane outlined that prior to going overseas all personnel were given the opportunity to make a will but he also pointed out that the making of a will was not compulsory.

The senior officer also confirmed that completed wills were forwarded for safekeeping to the Office of the Head Chaplain or the relevant Diocesan Secretariat.

Lt Col Minihane further confirmed that the force had no information on Fr Molloy's will: "In Fr Molloy's case, NO will was forwarded to the Office of the Head Chaplain, nor is there any record of an Officer of the Western Command having forwarded such a will to the Diocesan Secretariat of the Diocese of Elphin."

###

Billy Molloy died in 1987 and Ian Maher, his nephew, became the new Administrator of Niall's estate. On 5 August 1987, he took out probate and the assets then stood at IR£26,183.44. They included IR£2,000 worth of unsold household goods, a IR£4,000 Toyota Carina, and IR£19,905 in deposit accounts.

With Ian at the helm, the campaign for justice for Fr Molloy ramped up, and each time he discovered new information and leads, he followed through. It seemed very odd to him that there was a clear note of a discussion with Niall in 1972 where he said who was in receipt of his will, and where it was. It would have been unlike Niall to claim he had done something when he had not, particularly something important and official.

Ian decided to pursue the matter of the will with the Diocese of Elphin in Sligo, where Bishop Dominic Conway was in charge.

Behind the scenes, the Bishop and Army Chaplain corresponded about Niall's will as they fielded several queries about its whereabouts.

On 25 March 1988, Bishop Conway wrote to the Army Chaplain, Monsignor Edward Dunne, approving his proposed response but also suggesting that the Chaplain include Lt Col Minhane's assertion that there was no record of Niall's will being forwarded to the Diocesan Secretariat of the Diocese of Elphin.

It appeared to be a request for a definite response to any question of Fr Molloy's will ever existing in the Diocesan Office at any time.

There was also a note from Monsignor Dunne attached to a copy of this letter: "Phone call from Bishop Conway approving my minute of 28ᵗʰ March 1988 but suggesting that para 4 of Lt Col Minihane's response to the Parliamentary Question of 14 Nov 1986 be included to strengthen case even further. This has now been done."

The following text became the official response to any enquiry about Niall's will:

"From Head Chaplain of Defence Forces Right Rev Monsignor Edward Dunne:

1. With regards to diocesan priests the normal practice is that they are asked to make a will and to deposit it with the diocesan secretary or inform him where it is located.
2. With regard to army chaplains, the established procedure is that prior to going on overseas service, each chaplain is asked to make a will and to deposit it with the Head Chaplain or inform him where it is located.
3. There is no record that Fr Molloy deposited any will with the Head Chaplain.

4. There is however on record a note signed by a Capt. Flannan Cleary who was then Officer in Charge Records Western Area dated 26/9/72 which contains the following reference: "Fr Molloy informs me that his will is held by (a priest), St. Mary's, Sligo."

In 1988, a new legal firm representing the Flynns sought clarification about Fr Molloy's will from the Department, which confirmed on 21 April that the only record available was a note stating the will made by Fr Molloy was held by a clerical colleague.

The new legal firm, however, continued to press the Department on the issue: "This matter is now of extreme urgency and importance as far as our clients are concerned. … We are satisfied beyond all reasonable doubt that the late Fr Molloy did make a will while a member of the Defence Forces and that therefore, the original thereof, or a copy thereof, should be available. It is inconceivable to us that it cannot be located…"

In a further follow up letter, the firm noted the background to the will: "You will undoubtedly be aware of the controversy which has arisen in relation to the affairs of the late Fr Niall Molloy involving our clients, Richard and Therese Flynn, and it is, therefore, of paramount importance that the fullest possible information is made available to us in our attempts to locate the original, or indeed, a copy of the will of the late Fr Niall Molloy."

Almost four decades on, there is still no trace of Niall's will. The present Bishop of Elphin, Rev Kevin Doran, is sympathetic to the Molloys' quest, and has conducted several searches for the document, but confirmed that there is no record of Niall's will ever being lodged with the Diocese.

In the absence of Niall's will, the full extent of his assets could never be established. Over the course of their business partnership, it is believed that Niall and Therese jointly owned up to 20 horses at any one time, in addition to land in the Athlone area. Most of the horses were registered in Therese's name only but some were registered in the priest's name and several went on to compete internationally at the Royal Dublin Society or RDS, the home of the Aga Khan trophy.

In show jumping entries and gymkhana results, the horses were often listed under 'Mrs R Flynn' although press reports reference Fr Molloy's stake in some of the contenders.

In the *Irish Times*, coverage of the 1975 RDS Spring Show recounts the success of one of Therese Flynn's jumpers, Beverage.

"It is interesting that the Rev Niall Molloy CC, who has an interest in Beverage, used also to have an interest in Lydican," the report stated.

"In fact Fr Molloy rode the horse himself at the Spring Show in Dublin some years ago," it added.

Among the jointly owned show jumpers were El Greco, Jamestown, Tobias, Beverage, Kilcoursey, Kenilworth, Raphael, Lydican, Lismoyney and Tibohen.

There was also Stepaside, which was registered in Therese's name but believed by the Molloy family to have been Niall's horse. He was sold weeks after Niall's death for the sum of IR£20,000 to an Italian buyer attending the Horse Show in August 1985.

The Flynn family, however, later claimed that only IR£7,000 of the agreed purchase price had been paid over as the new owner refused to pay the balance owing because the horse was later found to have a heart defect.

In the end, the Flynns maintained that no profit was made from Stepaside's sale because of mounting veterinary bills of between IR£7,000-£10,000 for the horse.

More than three decades since the priest's death, the full extent of assets jointly owned by Fr Molloy and Mrs Flynn remains unclear.

Some critical documentation, such as bank records, have been lost since the death of Ian Maher, who had acted as administrator for Fr Molloy's estate in the 1980s.

Unlike today, most records were not computerised at this time, adding to the difficulty in tracking down documents.

Chapter 12
THE TIMELINE

The timeline of events and what really happened in Kilcoursey House on the Sunday night of 7 July 1985 and into the following morning remain shrouded in mystery.

The only account given was that of Richard Flynn, a narrative of events that appeared implausible and which was never tested or challenged. While Therese Flynn made two statements and testified at the inquest, her evidence shed little light on events as she suffered memory loss.

There is one key timestamp in Richard's statement: that it was midnight when he, Therese and Niall retired to the master bedroom for drinks and to continue their conversation.

The rest of his statement loosely describes the sequence of events but it is not specific in relation to the time they took place.

This was the only statement that Richard gave to Gardaí. It was based on a 20-minute interview with Inspector Monaghan in the early hours of 8 July. The businessman declined to speak to Gardaí thereafter and the Inspector's memo of interview was subsequently submitted by Mr Flynn's solicitor as his de facto statement. Richard also refused to be questioned by Gardaí about the land deal and monies owing to Niall. When his case went to court, Judge Frank Roe's intervention to cut the trial short relieved him of any obligation to give evidence about what happened.

Other witnesses who were present in Kilcoursey House that night and early morning helped to fill out the details of the timeline, although their testimonies also raised several discrepancies, in particular, about the comings and goings at Kilcoursey House that evening.

The remaining members of the Flynn family were not questioned by Gardaí as part of the investigation. Instead, facilitated by the law at the time, they provided witness statements through the family solicitor on 14 July, which in the end removed the opportunity for Gardaí to test their testimony.

In any criminal investigation the timeline of events is critical. In the Molloy case, the timeline and any discrepancies within it, take on even greater significance when considering the fresh medical evidence obtained in 1988 and the potential evidential value of Fr Molloy's watch.

The medical evidence, which has been corroborated by several pathologists and medical experts over the years, suggests the priest took hours rather than minutes to die.

Evidence that Niall's broken watch was stuck at 10.40 also prompts fresh questions over the timeline of events and whether, in fact, he may have been assaulted much earlier than stated by Richard.

Given the critical nature of the timeline, we have detailed the possible timings of events that night in the following table. The timeline is based on statements given to Gardaí or the Flynn family solicitor, as well as witness testimony given at Richard's trial and the subsequent inquest into Niall's death.

Time	Evidence	Witness	Source
7pm	Richard, Therese and Niall leave Kilcoursey for Goodbodys	Maureen Parkes	Trial
7pm	Richard, Therese and Niall leave Kilcoursey for Goodbodys	Zandra Flynn	Statement
7pm	Richard, Therese and Niall leave Kilcoursey for Goodbodys	Anita Flynn	Statement
7pm	Richard, Therese and Niall leave Kilcoursey for Goodbodys	Therese Flynn	Garda statement (hospital)
7pm	James Lowry speaks to Niall in the kitchen at Kilcoursey House – Therese is also present in the house	James Lowry, groom at Kilcoursey House	Statement and trial
7.30pm	Richard, Therese and Niall leave Kilcoursey for Goodbodys	Maureen Parkes	Statement
7.30pm	Richard, Therese and Niall arrive at Goodbodys	Douglas Goodbody, neighbour	Statement and trial
9pm	Therese is in the kitchen at Kilcoursey House	James Lowry, groom at Kilcoursey House	Trial
9pm	Wedding group leave for White's pub	Ralph Parkes	Statement
9.15pm	Richard, Therese, Niall return to Kilcoursey from Goodbodys	Therese Flynn	Garda statement (hospital)
9.15pm	Auntie May in bed	Therese Flynn	Garda statement (hospital)

Time	Evidence	Witness	Source
9.15pm	Maureen and Ann leave to go to Tober House (not White's)	Therese Flynn	Garda statement (hospital)
9.20pm	Richard, Therese and Fr Niall leave Goodbodys	Douglas Goodbody, neighbour	Trial
9.20pm	James Lowry speaks to Therese in the hallway of Kilcoursey	James Lowry, groom at Kilcoursey House	Statement
9.30pm	Richard, Therese and Niall return home from Goodbodys	Therese Flynn	Statement to solicitor
9.30pm	Auntie May up but went to bed	Therese Flynn	Statement to solicitor
9.35pm	On their way to White's pub the small wedding party meets Richard, Therese and Niall on their way back from Goodbodys and stop to chat briefly	David Flynn	Statement
9.40pm	The wedding party leaves Kilcoursey for White's pub	Anita Flynn	Statement
9.45pm	Richard, Therese, Niall return to Kilcoursey from Goodbodys	Maureen Parkes	Trial and statement
12am	The wedding party leaves White's pub in Clara for Tober House	Maureen Parkes	Trial
12am	Auntie May goes to bed	May Quinn	Statement and inquest

Time	Evidence	Witness	Source
12am	Richard and Therese went to bed and Niall followed up to their bedroom for a chat	Richard Flynn	Statement
12.30-.45am	Wedding party leaves Tober House	David Flynn	Statement
12.30-.40am	Wedding party leaves Tober House	Anita Flynn	Statement
12.50am	Wedding party leaves Tober House	Zandra Flynn	Statement
1am	Fr Deignan receives a call from Richard to come to Kilcoursey	Fr Deignan	Trial, statement and inquest
1am	Wedding party leaves Tober House	Ralph Parkes	Statement
1am	Wedding party leaves Tober House	Maureen Parkes	Trial
1am	Wedding party arrives back at Kilcoursey	Anita Flynn	Statement
1am	Wedding party arrives back at Kilcoursey	Maureen Parkes	Statement
1.05am	Fr Deignan arrives at Kilcoursey House	Fr Deignan	Trial
1.10am	David Flynn goes to bed in Tober House	David Flynn	Statement
1.10am	Zandra Flynn in kitchen in Kilcoursey	Zandra Flynn	Statement
1.10am	Maureen, Zandra and Anita arrive back to Kilcoursey	Fr Deignan	Inquest
1.20am	Fr Deignan finishes anointing Fr Molloy	Fr Deignan	Inquest

Time	Evidence	Witness	Source
1.40am	David Flynn receives a call from Ralph Parkes about Fr Molloy	David Flynn	Statement
1.50am	Fr Deignan and Zandra Flynn arrive at doctor's house in Kilbeggan	Dr O'Sullivan	Trial
2am	Dr O'Sullivan is woken by Fr Deignan and Zandra Flynn at home	Dr O'Sullivan	Statement and inquest
2am	Dr O'Sullian arrives at Kilcoursey House	Dr O'Sullivan	Trial and inquest
2am	Dr O'Sullian arrives at Kilcoursey House	Maureen Parkes	Trial
3am	Dr O'Sullivan leaves Kilcoursey for Tullamore Hospital	Dr O'Sullivan	Trial and inquest
3am	Dr O'Sullivan arrives at Tullamore Hospital with Therese	Dr O'Sullivan	Inquest
3.00	Therese admitted to Tullamore Hospital	Maureen Parkes	Statement
3.00	James Lowry returns to Kilcoursey House from Tullamore – Zandra, Ralph, David and Ann are there	James Lowry, groom at Kilcoursey House	Trial and statement
3.15am	Therese is admitted to Tullamore Hospital	Dr Peter Grealy, Tullamore Hospital	Inquest
3.15am	James Lowry sees Fr Deignan in the kitchen at Kilcoursey House	James Lowry, groom at Kilcoursey House	Trial

Time	Evidence	Witness	Source
3.15am	Fr Deignan calls to Sgt. Kevin Forde at Clara Garda Station	Garda Sergeant Kevin Forde	Trial and statement
3.20am	James Lowry speaks to Fr Deignan in the kitchen about football	James Lowry, groom at Kilcoursey House	Statement
3.30am	Sgt. Kevin Forde arrives at Kilcoursey House, meets Dr O'Sullivan	Garda Sergeant Kevin Forde	Trial and statement
4am	James Lowry leaves Kilcoursey House to go outside	James Lowry, groom at Kilcoursey House	Trial and statement
4.25am	Inspector Thomas Monaghan arrives at Kilcoursey House	Garda Inspector Tom Monaghan	Trial / statement
6.30am	Dr Dorman – Niall's doctor – phones the Flynns	Maureen Parkes	Statement

Where there are only marginal differences between the stated times, allowances can be made for some human error in recalling events.

Some of the inherent discrepancies in the timeline, however, demand closer attention and scrutiny, in particular the following:

- Therese gave two statements; one was given to Gardaí on 9 July at Tullamore Hospital and the second was made on 14 July and provided through her solicitor. Between these two recollections alone, Therese provided different times for when she, Richard and Niall left Kilcoursey for their neighbours the Goodbodys, when they returned, and when she and Auntie May went to bed.

- There are also discrepancies in Fr Deignan's evidence. His statement and the testimony he gave at the trial and inquest were at odds as to the time he was called by Richard, the time he arrived at Kilcoursey, the time he returned to the parochial house for his glasses, and the arrival of the wedding party from Tober House. For instance, he stated there was nobody else apart from Richard and Therese in the house when he administered the Last Rites to Niall between 1am and 1.20am, yet members of the wedding party stated they had returned to Kilcoursey by 1am.

- Another neighbour of the Flynns, Brian Sheridan, gave a statement to Gardaí as part of the Serious Crime Review Team investigation that Niall spoke to his daughter that evening, after she had competed at the Blessington Horse Show earlier that day. Niall was on his usual jaunt around Clara on his horse and trap when he stopped to chat. She recalled it was between 9pm and 9.30pm and it was still bright. Her statement contrasts with the timeline put forward by members of the Flynn family, that it was anywhere from 9.15pm to 9.45pm when Niall and Richard and Therese returned from the Goodbodys to Kilcoursey.

- The evidence of May Quinn, an elderly aunt of the Flynns who was residing at Kilcoursey, also begs some questions. According to Therese, Auntie May, as she was known, was in bed or went to bed shortly after they returned from the Goodbodys (anywhere from 9.15-9.45pm). Miss Quinn, in her own statement, however, said she was playing the card game 'Patience' while Richard, Therese and Niall chatted in the sitting room. She further stated that she went to bed at around midnight when she observed Niall going upstairs with a glass of milk and that she did not see or hear any disturbance after that.

- There are also questions over the comings and goings of the three parties on the night: Richard, Therese and Niall; the wedding party; and Ann and Maureen Flynn. Conflicting statements over the time that the wedding party, which comprised David, Anita and Zandra Flynn, Ralph Parkes, and four close friends, went to White's pub in the local village raise some doubt over the timeline of events.

- The time that Therese was taken to Tullamore Hospital on the night raises further questions. The time that Dr O'Sullivan, Maureen and Anita Flynn left Kilcoursey to take Therese to hospital stretches from 2.45am to 3.00am. Depending on whose statement is considered, Therese was admitted sometime between 3am and 3.30am, yet Dr O'Sullivan was back at Kilcoursey House by 3.30am to answer the door to Sgt Kevin Forde.

Fr Molloy was not a fan of ostentation or shows of wealth, but he did like good quality. Dressing for the after-wedding lunch in Kilcoursey, he put on his favourite watch, a Swiss Favre-Leuba. There was nothing particularly special about the gold face and bracelet, but it was solid, discreet and kept perfect time.

For the Molloy family, it was the smoking gun. Within days of Niall's death, the expensive watch was returned to the family. It appeared to be broken and the hands were stuck at 10.40.

The timeline of events in Kilcoursey House took on even greater significance given the time on the broken watch and they believed it to be a potentially vital piece of evidence.

Valued at around IR£200, the gold watch was among the priest's personal effects handled by Gardaí and detailed as part of the post-mortem process and chain of evidence.

But it was only after Richard Flynn's truncated trial in 1986, that the watch became a contentious issue when the Molloy family raised it in a *Today Tonight* programme on RTE that aired before the inquest into Niall's death.

One of Niall's nieces, Liz Molloy from Castlerea, said that she had noticed the glass on the face was broken and the watch had stopped when it was returned to the family.

As such a valued and personal item belonging to their lost brother and uncle, the family decided to have the watch repaired at a local jewellers. Unfortunately, what the family thought was a good deed in honour of Niall would ultimately spoil any chance of the watch being used to inform the time of his death.

In response to the Molloy family's concerns, and given the watch's potential evidential value, Gardaí moved to set the record straight on how the watch was handled.

Weeks later at the priest's inquest, several Gardaí attached to the Technical Bureau made a series of supplementary statements about the condition of the watch at the time of his post-mortem.

Dr Harbison estimated that the time of death could have been any time between 11pm on 7 July and 5am on 8 July. "I would not like to say which side of midnight death occurred," he said.

While the new Garda evidence cast doubt over the evidential value of the watch, the Molloy family were certain it was broken and stopped at 10.40 when it was returned to them, along with Niall's two sets of car keys, cash, and a miraculous medal and chain.

Years later, as part of the SCRT probe, the Castlerea jeweller who repaired Fr Molloy's watch, told Gardaí that the second hand was trapped in the cracked glass which had stopped the watch mechanism. The battery was flat but otherwise the watch was in working order.

Unfortunately, any potential evidential value offered by the watch was lost when it was returned by Gardaí to the family, which in turn broke the chain of evidence.

If the watch was in fact broken and stopped working during the altercation at Kilcoursey, this was almost five hours before Gardaí arrived on the scene.

Add to this, new medical evidence brought forward in 1988 – suggesting that Fr Molloy survived for hours before dying – and it raises even more critical questions and doubts over the timeline of events presented.

The more recent 2015 McGinn report into the Molloy case concluded that Gardaí should have investigated the condition of Niall's watch before returning it to his family after the post-mortem.

Chief Superintendent Christopher Mangan acknowledged that the watch was a key issue for Fr Molloy's relatives.

"The family believed that a technical examination of the watch should have taken place and were obviously concerned that the time that the watch showed what they believe was the time of the actual death of Fr Molloy," he said.

In his assessment of the case, the watch may have proven useful. Superintendent Mangan added: "If we were told that Fr Molloy had unfortunately had the injuries inflicted, let's say at 10.40, which was the time on the watch and then put onto that another four hours, six hours. Well, then people who arrived after that would have questions to answer but it wasn't known; it wasn't established in evidence for the investigators."

Decades later, some who were involved in the original Garda investigation believe that the watch was central to the case.

The missed opportunity to analyse and forensically examine Fr Molloy's watch is something that still haunts retired Garda Sergeant Kevin Forde today. "The main regret that I have is that I didn't draw attention to the watch. It was an oversight on my part," he explained.

Chapter 13
THE MEDICAL EVIDENCE

Since 1985, several medical experts have come to the same damning conclusion – that Fr Niall Molloy had survived for hours rather than minutes after he was assaulted and beaten.

Their examinations were carried out independent of each other over several decades and lend unequivocal support to the State Pathologist's conclusion that the priest died from head injuries and not a heart attack.

In his post-mortem examination of Fr Molloy's body in Tullamore Hospital, Dr John Harbison was both thorough and meticulous. He concluded that the cause of death was head injuries.

Despite this firm conclusion, a chink of doubt over the medical evidence was raised at Richard Flynn's trial. It was enough to see the trial collapse and Mr Flynn walk free from court.

The medical evidence, then and now, however cuts through any suggestion that Niall died of a heart attack, as we detail here.

On 6 August 1985, the post-mortem report included the following detail:

The Head

1. A group of lacerations on the left side of the mouth
2. A group of bruises on the nose with an abrasion on the right
3. An area of spotty bruising over the right cheekbone
4. Abrasions on the right ear
5. A laceration on the shaft of the lower jaw on the left side
6. A group of abrasions to the left of the midline on the tip of the chin.

The Upper Limbs

1. An area of faded bruising on the left forearm

The Lower Limbs

1. Bruises with fading edges on both knees and on the middle of the left shin
2. An abrasion with a lower skin flap on the left thigh, 1.5" below the scrotum
3. An abrasion on the surface of the right lower leg above and behind the medial malleolus (inner ankle)

1. A few petechiae (tiny spots of bleeding under the skin) on the inner surface of the lower lid of the right eye.

On examining the body internally, Dr Harbison noted the following:

The Head – The skull and dura were intact. There was bleeding into the right temporalis muscle and further areas of bleeding. There was a diffuse thin subdural haemorrhage, clotted but fresh, and bore no evidence of any membrane. Evidence of bleeding in different areas of the brain. The trachea and larynx contained white froth.

Lungs – Both lungs were grossly oedematous, with the right weighing 950 grammes and the left 1,000 grammes. No evidence of an underlying disease or embolism.

Heart – The pericardium was healthy. The heart externally was normal in size with two white fibrotic patches on its anterior surface. It weighed 400 grammes, the upper limit of normal for a man of his stature. The left ventricle showed slight hypertrophy (thickening of the wall) and a section of myocardium showed an area of possible scar tissue, not more than one centimetre across. It was otherwise healthy in appearance. The coronary arteries, although showing traces of atheroma (build-up of materials that adhere to arteries), were patent. Heart valves normal. Some calcification in the abdominal part of the aorta. Oesophagus normal.

During the post-mortem, samples of tissue from several body organs were taken and retained for laboratory analysis. Samples of brain tissue were preserved in formalin and cut into small sections and stained on glass slides for microscopic examination.

As part of the post-mortem into Fr Molloy's death, the State Pathologist sought the opinion of a neuropathologist who he invited to examine slides of the priest's brain tissue.

The State Pathologist met with Dr Michael Farrell, a Consultant Neuropathologist, on 30 July 1985, and their examination concluded that a section of the brain showed acute swelling.

In the State Pathologist's final post-mortem report he concluded that Fr Molloy died late on the night of 7 July or in the very early hours of 8 July 1985 due to acute brain swelling and acute subdural haemorrhage, arising from multiple injuries to the head, neck and face.

The distribution of the injuries, Dr Harbison said, was consistent with the deceased receiving five, six, or more blows, by a fist. The violence was insufficient to fracture any facial bones.

Dr Harbison also identified pulmonary oedema or the waterlogging of Fr Molloy's lungs. This, he concluded, was most likely associated with the head injuries sustained, a phenomenon known as "cerebral lung", which in turn gave rise to the froth seen exuding from Niall's mouth.

Inhalation of vomit or acute heart failure were alternative explanations but the pathological evidence weighed towards head injuries as the cause of death, he found.

The medical evidence in relation to Niall's heart was weak by comparison and there was no evidence that he inhaled vomit or any other material.

Dr Harbison found that the enlargement of Niall's heart was minimal, even within the upper limits of normal. There was no evidence of hypertension or high blood pressure and it was not clear what caused the slight thickening of one of the heart chambers.

The State Pathologist concluded that these observations did not detract from his opinion that the primary cause of death was due to head injuries.

His examination also found that Niall had no injury of a defensive or offensive nature on his arms or hands. A fading bruise on Niall's left forearm seemed to pre-date the final assault on Fr Molloy.

Summing up his evidence at Richard's trial, the State Pathologist said: "Fr Niall Molloy, in my opinion, died of acute brain swelling or the effects of acute brain swelling and acute subdural haemorrhage, both resulting from multiple injuries to his head and neck, principally to his face."

Dr Harbison told the court he found no evidence of Niall having a heart attack.

"I examined the area of apparent scar tissue in the heart under the microscope and confirmed it but could not find any evidence of recent muscle tissue death, that is of a recent infarct or heart attack."

"The degree of coronary artery disease in this man was not very great," he added, as he reiterated his opinion that the primary cause of death was head injury.

The State Pathologist was more explicit in his evidence at the subsequent inquest in July 1986 when he said: "No evidence of recent infarction was noted."

He also discounted counter arguments put forward by fellow pathologist Dr Declan Gilsenan at the inquest, on behalf of the Flynn family.

Dr Harbison rebuffed Dr Gilsenan's alternative views on the cause of death and elaborated further on his opinion – that Niall died from head injuries and not a heart attack. In the end, the inquest jury accepted Dr Harbison's evidence.

Two years after the inquest into Niall's death, the Molloy family were approached by a medical expert offering to carry out an independent assessment of the available evidence.

Dermot Hourihane, a Professor of Histopathology at Trinity College Dublin, was moved to offer the family his medical expertise after he saw an RTE *Today Tonight* report into the death.

On his examination, Professor Hourihane agreed with the State Pathologist's assessment that the injuries to Niall's jaw were as a result of being kicked when lying down.

Commenting further on Niall's injuries, Professor Hourihane concluded: "I also believe that the small abrasion of the skin of the inside of one thigh is suggestive of a blow struck while the deceased was lying on the ground and there is a description of bleeding around the outside of one kidney which is very suggestive of a severe blow to his back, probably a kick, and also probably executed while he was lying on the ground with a flexed back or in a bent position."

He also agreed with Dr Harbison that there was unconvincing evidence of underlying heart disease and that death was due to pulmonary oedema or the water-logging of Niall's lungs as a result of brain swelling.

The extent of bleeding, he found, indicated that Fr Molloy had lived for hours rather than minutes after the initial assault.

A third medical opinion was ventured by Dr John Dinn, a consultant neuropathologist at St James's Hospital, who also examined the available materials. His report concluded that the extent of bleeding would not occur within a one-hour period and that Niall did not die suddenly.

These fresh findings encouraged the Molloy family to bring this medical evidence to Gardaí in the hope of having the case reopened in 1988.

In the family's mind, there was now robust medical evidence that the priest had lived for hours after the attack – established in the inquest and by new independent medical opinions – which would justify a fresh review of how Niall died. Despite the new medical evidence, their calls for a new inquiry met a dead end.

In the intervening years, the Molloy family carefully safeguarded the slides of Niall's brain tissue, the only medical evidence now available.

They were also examined as part of the Serious Crime Review Team investigation in 2011.

The slides were reviewed by Dr Francesca Brett, a Consultant Neuropathologist at Beaumont Hospital, whose opinion was even more damning and upsetting in terms of the estimated length of time Fr Molloy may have survived after being attacked.

In her assessment, Dr Brett concluded the priest may have survived for anywhere between six and 24 hours.

Dr Michael Farrell also reviewed the slides again and, as before, concluded Niall survived for hours before dying.

Again, this new medical evidence was relayed to Gardaí. In 2020, as part of the TV documentary, Professor Jack Crane, the former State Pathologist for Northern Ireland, reviewed the slides, post-mortem report, statements and transcripts.

As Dr Harbison had done, Professor Crane considered what Niall's heart and lungs could offer in terms of medical evidence.

He found that Niall's heart muscle was "normal and healthy" but also found an area of scar tissue. "In the past, he suffered an insult to the heart, months or years before his death."

If this earlier trauma was a factor in causing a heart attack, Fr Molloy would have collapsed and died instantly, but this was not the case.

"What isn't clear from Dr Harbison's report is the mechanism; how did he get the head injuries? That's why it's important to have an open mind," Professor Crane told the documentary.

On Niall's lungs, Professor Crane said he observed that the lung tissue was normal but there was evidence of blood in the air spaces, suggesting he survived for some time before dying.

"What's important to note is that if someone dies rapidly, they don't have time to inhale blood, but with an injury where the person is still breathing and inhaling, it indicates that death is not immediate. One has to be alive to inhale and it takes time for the blood to be inhaled into the lungs, maybe an hour or two," he remarked.

He added that the water-logging of Niall's lungs would not have happened quickly: "It takes time to develop and is not seen in a sudden death."

The former State Pathologist for Northern Ireland examined samples of Niall's brain tissue, which also offered evidence that the priest survived for hours rather than minutes after sustaining his injuries.

He observed that the brain tissue was swollen as a result of trauma or injury, concurring with Dr Harbison's evidence.

"In a rapid death, there is no swelling or accumulation of blood, as it develops over a period of time," Professor Crane said.

He added that the swelling of the brain was the most common form of death after a head injury but that treatment in hospital can increase the chance of survival if urgent medical attention is sought.

"The swelling can be brought down and the patient might be fine, but if there is damage to the brain, it can have a different outcome," he said.

"In Niall's case, there wasn't a significant amount of bleeding over the brain – in that case, the doctors would make a subdural hole in the skull and evacuate the blood – so treatment would have been fairly straightforward in any hospital," he added.

On assessing the available evidence, Professor Crane concluded, like other medical experts before him, that Fr Molloy did not die immediately: "Fr Niall didn't die instantly or quickly; death was not rapid. He sustained injuries and survived unconscious for a period of time, possibly hours. Two factors that indicate that period of survival are the blood inhaled and the fluid accumulated. His death was not due to one blow, but a number of them".

Over the past three decades there was broad agreement among all of the medical experts who assessed the available medical evidence – there was no evidence of a heart attack and Fr Molloy survived for a number of hours after being beaten and possibly kicked.

Chapter 14
THE FORENSIC EVIDENCE

"Therese was a crime scene. She was the crime scene that got away." This was the conclusion of Angela Doyle, Crime Scene Specialist and former member of Merseyside Police.

More questions than answers remained after the SCRT investigation and the McGinn report, so as part of the TV documentary, the bedroom in Kilcoursey House was recreated to test the available evidence, with fresh eyes.

The set was built to the exact specifications of the Garda technical drawings, forensic records, statements, and sight of the original crime scene photos; by replicating it exactly, any new findings would therefore have a high level of credibility.

Our 'fresh eyes' were the above-mentioned Angela Doyle, former Northern Ireland State Pathologist Professor Jack Crane OBE, and Forensic Psychologist Ciara Staunton. Each is a leader in their field and approached the task with absolute objectivity, impartiality, and an open mind.

Placing themselves on the bedroom set, they could see in context what the statements and reports claimed, from where Richard and Therese Flynn and Fr Niall Molloy sat, to the streak of blood across the bedroom floor, to the blood patterns on the walls and elsewhere.

THE ROOM

Angela was first to take an overall view of the scene. Her initial thoughts were that it was remarkably tidy given the apparent violent altercation that had occurred – something the State Pathologist had also commented on in his post-mortem report. There were items of clothing thrown over chairs or the bedstead, with the odd shoe and sock on the floor, but nothing was overturned or disturbed. There was no sign of an altercation, apart from the unmissable eight-foot blood streak on the cream carpet. The other blood stains, such as those on the walls, skirting boards, doors, pictures, television and bedclothes were not immediately visible and several were described as 'minute' in the forensic report by Gardaí.

"We like to go in to view a crime scene in what we call 'The Golden Hour', the hour just after a crime has been committed. You get a feel for the place that you don't get from photos or state-ments," Angela explained.

Assessing the reconstructed bedroom, she added: "The level of detail in this room is phenomenal. What it has allowed us to do is get a real perspective on what happened. You'll notice there's nothing disturbed or out of place. Unfortunately a number of hours had passed before the authorities were called.

"People were in and out of the house during this time which gave ample opportunity for changes to be made to the original scene. Crime scene examination is honest and objective. If anybody wanted to alter the scene they could have done. We can only comment on what this scene tells us now."

THE BED

According to Therese's statement, she and Richard were in bed, and Niall was sitting at the foot of it. In Richard's statement, he got out of bed to go down for a drink, and Niall was "sitting in the room" when the businessman was attacked by them both. However, in the Garda drawings, there was no chair in the room that was positioned for the chat Richard described. The chairs were either against the wall and covered in discarded clothes and blankets, or too far away for Niall to be heard, so Therese's statement fits with the layout and findings of the Gardaí.

Physically pacing out the action, according to witness statements, Angela sat where Therese was supposed to be, indicated by the cosmetics and ornaments on the bedside locker. Professor Crane sat where Richard was, and Ciara sat at the end of the bed, where it was likely that Niall sat.

Instantly, the intimate physical closeness of three adults on a five foot by six foot bed was evident. It felt uncomfortable, as it would be for anyone who was less than an exceptionally good friend, confidante or partner.

Commenting on the scenario, Ciara questioned the dynamic between the three long-time friends: "This is a very private space. A husband would only allow a relationship to form when there's no threat to the marital bed."

On the basis of Richard's statement, if he was attacked by Therese and Niall when he had got out of bed, all three of them would have had to have been standing.

Therese would have got out of bed on her side and come around to be close enough for Richard to strike her.

The likely position of the trio in the bedroom is important in assessing the scene and possible events, the experts suggested.

Ciara said it would be a natural reaction for individuals to stand to defend or attack when they go into 'fight or flight' mode when under threat.

"If this was premeditated, you'd expect to find a weapon or piece of equipment in the room, and there was no evidence of this. The high emotional charge would fit with using fists. If premeditated, it would be different psychologically. It would be more violent initially, as the criminal wants to be in control and have the upper hand," she explained.

Professor Crane also noted that Fr Molloy did not have any defensive or offensive injuries, raising a doubt over what may have occurred in the bedroom. "You might expect to see injuries to Fr Niall's knuckles and you might expect to see injuries elsewhere. There were no offensive injuries to indicate he was involved in fighting with someone, and no defensive injuries to suggest he has tried to defend himself. If you put your arms up, you find bruising along the arm."

Ciara also raised the question of whether Niall may have been surprised by his attacker: "Even the gentlest of people would have an instinctive physical reaction to an imminent attack. So, was he surprised? Was he struck from behind? Did Richard come from behind and punch him? There must have been a sudden outburst that Fr Niall was unaware of. Did he turn his back to walk away, and that's when it happened? Could Therese have hit him and it was so unexpected, he didn't respond?"

Professor Crane said: "There was bruising on the undersurface at the back of the scalp, like banging his head on a hard, unyielding surface, and he could have remained there after that. Given the bloodstains on the bedclothes, it's likely Fr Niall has been on the bed at some point, if that blood is his."

If Fr Molloy was sitting on the bed facing Richard, the experts did not rule out the possibility that Therese could have come around and struck him from behind. If this blow surprised, dazed or knocked him unconscious, then the bloodstains found in that area of the room made sense.

THE ACT OF CONTRITION

Richard's testimony about what happened oscillated between knocking the priest out completely with the first few blows, and Niall getting up from the floor, only for Richard to strike him again, rendering him unconscious.

When Richard realised he had knocked Niall and his wife out, he went to the bathroom for water to splash on them. When he splashed water on Therese, she revived, but Niall did not. At this point, Richard realised Niall was in trouble. He recalled that Niall had a "heart condition" so he recited the Act of Contrition into his ear.

On this aspect of the evidence, Ciara commented: "So, after knocking him out and then realising he may have gone too far, Richard then says a prayer into his ear. Is this remorse, or guilt on Richard's behalf?"

THE BLOOD

Evidence provided at Niall's inquest detailed his injuries, a long bloody drag mark on the carpet, as well as spatters of blood throughout the room.

Under questioning at the inquest, Detective Keating explained the different types of blood spatter found in the bedroom and ensuite. Blood coming from a particular direction has a small tail which would be the direction away from which it came. Blood dropping on a surface would have a reasonable round pattern. Blood from an object striking severely enough to make a laceration would have a sunburst pattern, with ray-like strokes emanating from the centre in all directions.

He noted where blood was present inside and outside the bedroom and whether it was diluted.

Also at the inquest, Richard suggested the injuries suffered by Niall – apart from the two or three blows he had inflicted with his fists – were from falling against the bedpost or TV, but the bedpost did not have any blood on it. The baseboard did, but it did not have a sunburst pattern that would result from someone falling against it, it was a blood pattern more associated with a wound bleeding and falling on the bed board. The TV had small splashes of blood on the screen and magazines that lay on top of it but it was not disturbed in the way that might be expected if a man of almost six feet in height fell against it.

Richard's own injuries were bruising to his upper arm and a mallet finger, from when he said he put out his hand to ward off a punch from Niall. The punch would have had to have landed on the top of his finger to give him that injury. But, as it was discovered in the post-mortem, Fr Molloy had no offensive or defensive injuries, there was no evidence of him attacking anyone, or defending himself against an attack, despite Richard's version of events.

The injury to Niall's left cheek was of particular note, according to Professor Crane: "This was not caused by a punch, but by a

THE KILLING OF FR NIALL MOLLOY

hard, unyielding surface, such as a sharp bedpost, but there was no corresponding bloodstain to explain this anywhere in the room."

"The severity of the wound and the ensuing bleeding would not be expected from a punch with a fist. This injury more likely was sustained while Fr Niall lay on the floor, rather than when he was standing. It would have been a kick, rather than a stamp, as there's no pattern bruising from the footwear, and it wouldn't cause a laceration," he added.

The inquest heard evidence from Gardaí that the blood patterns suggested that Fr Molloy's body was flipped over so that he lay on his back.

Angela agreed: "Blood under the door knob of the closet travelling upwards from the direction of the lower hinge could have been from a blow being struck or an implement being wielded from down on the floor, or if the body was quickly turned over into the position it was found. If a weapon was used, or a foot kicked Fr Niall on the ground, there would be minute spatters of blood upwards."

THE DRAG MARK

In Richard's evidence at the inquest, he could not remember if he had dragged Fr Molloy from the bed to the door, nor did he notice the injuries to his face. When he said the Act of Contrition into his left ear, Niall's head was turned over on his right side, but his injuries were on the left side of his face, clear to see. At that stage, his pulse was very slow, according to Richard.

In her statement, Therese said she did not notice any blood from the priest's wounds, or the streak across the floor, but did see blood from Niall's ear.

When asked about Niall's injuries at the inquest she said: "I didn't see any sign of violence or blood. My brain was very addled and I was dazed."

Therese conceded she herself "could easily have" dragged Niall across the floor, as she raised him up to see what was wrong.

Looking at the recreated streak of blood on the carpet, Professor Crane suggested it was likely to have stemmed from the priest's facial injuries.

"We don't know how he ended up in this position. For the blood to be on the carpet in such a way, Fr Niall either dragged himself or staggered across the room towards the door, or he was dragged, face down. He was lying for a period of time, long enough to leave this amount of blood," he said.

He added there was a question over a clean area of about two feet between the drag mark and Fr Molloy's body and how this may have come about: "He would need to be lifted to this position from the end of the drag mark. One individual could possibly drag rather than lift him and it would be easier if there's more than one person involved to lift a body".

The experts also considered the possibility that Fr Molloy was dragged in the opposite direction, from the door to the bed, and then carried back again.

Angela suggested it was not clear cut from the available evidence: "Was he dragged over to the door to get him out? Or was he dragged from the door to the bed? And then carried back to the door to get rid of him? We assume he was dragged from the bed to the door and that caused the blood streak, but perhaps it's the other way around."

The second reason for considering this scenario was the other, unproven, rumour that has circulated since 1985 – that Fr Molloy was attacked downstairs, taken by surprise and struck with a sharp object and carried, unconscious, through the house and upstairs to the bedroom, to make it look like a crime of passion.

The discovery of a bloodstain on the newel post of the banister at the top of the stairs, as part of a forensic examination of the house, added to the speculation.

THE TOWEL

When Sgt Garda Kevin Forde first examined the scene, Niall had an orange towel over his face. The crime scene photos showed bloodstains on Niall's shirt but no line of blood from the wounds to the staining.

Garda evidence also pointed to the possibility that Niall was cleaned up, something Dr O'Sullivan also commented on when he arrived at Kilcoursey to attend to him.

In the view of the experts, the towel may be relevant in assessing what possibly happened, from either a practical or psychological point of view.

Professor Crane noted the practical implications of using a towel to cover Niall's face: "There was blood leaking from a wound on his face. If someone is trying to move the body they wouldn't want blood on the floor, walls, or themselves."

Ciara, however, suggested there may be psychological reasons behind the towel's placement. "Where there is a close personal relationship, covering the face specifically removes the identifying aspect. The perpetrator or witness didn't want to see what had been done to someone they knew so well," she remarked.

"It allows you to get to the next step. What next? What do we do here now?" she added.

FORENSIC EVIDENCE

Detective Garda Keating assisted the State Pathologist Dr Harbison with the gathering of items on and surrounding the body of Niall, and attended the post-mortem in Tullamore Hospital later that day.

From the scene, amongst other things, he took:

- Debris from the neck of Fr Molloy
- Cotton wool and a tissue from near the body
- A clear plastic box and top from near the body
- Two samples of the bloodstained carpet
- A button from a flower box lying against a chair
- Cigars from the bedside locker near the window (Richard's side of the bed)
- Sellotape lifts from the bottom sheet of the bed
- The towel that had been covering Fr Molloy's face
- A brown jacket from near the foot of Fr Molloy's body
- All the bedclothes and duvet
- Clothing and a magazine from the foot of the bed
- Underwear from under the left pillow
- A blue towel from an armchair
- Bloodstained magazine from the top of the TV

Blood swabs were taken from these locations, numbered, and returned to the National Forensics Laboratory for analysis, 32 in all.

Blood samples were not taken from Richard and Therese until 15 July 1985 when Det. Sgt. Thomas Dunne, from the Investigation Section, called to Dr O'Sullivan's surgery and met them there. He cautioned them and they both consented to having their blood taken, Richard saying he had nothing to hide.

CLOTHING

Det Garda Noel Lynagh, of Tullamore Garda Station, attended the scene early on the morning of 8 July, as Richard Flynn was speaking to Inspector Thomas Monaghan and Sgt Kevin Forde and Det Sgt Dunne.

At 5.30am, shortly after the interview ended, Det. Lynagh met Richard in a bedroom, where he showed him his hands. Det Garda Lynagh saw bruises on the end joints of his right index finger and right thumb, around the nail.

Richard agreed these injuries were as a result of his hitting Niall, saying "I hit him under the chin, I know I did" and making an upward striking motion with his fist. Garda Lynagh also noticed two small, fresh-looking scratches on the edge of his left hand, but Richard made no comment about them. He readily gave Garda Lynagh the clothes he was wearing – pyjamas, dressing-gown, shoes and socks.

At 8am, the Detective Garda was approached by Ralph Parkes and Richard Flynn to say the clothes Mr Flynn had handed over were not those he had been wearing the night before.

Mr Parkes brought Garda Lynagh to the main hallway, where the top and bottom of a man's pyjamas lay. Richard confirmed they were what he was wearing when the incident with Niall occurred. They had been in a wash-basket in an upstairs bathroom.

On 12 July, Det. Sgt Dunne handed Garda Lynagh a night-dress, dressing gown and blanket from Therese, reportedly from when she was brought to Tullamore Hospital. Later that day, Garda Lynagh delivered all of these items to the Forensic Science

Laboratory. At the trial and inquest, there was no indication that the shoes and socks Richard gave to Garda Lynagh had been forensically examined. They, and many more items collected for processing, were not listed in the forensic report.

FINGERPRINTS

Detectives took finger and palm prints at the scene, but they did not appear to be identified or matched. Today no forensic samples or exhibits are available.

WHO SLEPT WHERE?

The available evidence also raised questions over which room was Niall's. As part of the Garda forensic investigation, Det. Garda Keating processed Room No. 9, as per the layout drawing, which was beside the master bedroom.

From this room, he took the following samples:

Carpet clipping from Stain No. 1

Carpet Clipping from Stain No. 2

Cigar from top of wardrobe

Pyjamas from the windowsill of the shower room opposite the door into the master bedroom

Blood from the newel post at the top of the stairs on the landing.

At the inquest, under examination, Garda Keating said Room No. 9 was the one Fr Molloy slept in.

Detective Garda Edwin Handcock, from the Ballistics section, processed another bedroom, Room No. 2, beside the master bedroom at the end of the house. He noted it contained a brass double bed, which was unmade. This bed was identified by the Mollloy family as Niall's, as it used to be in his room in Carrowroe House. Another individual who occasionally worked at Kilcoursey also described the room at the end of the house as being Niall's.

Two pillows were propped up against the head of the bed, in the centre. The table lamp on the left bedside locker was still switched on, and also there was a glass of milk on a silver ashtray. An empty packet of Ritmeester Pikeur mild cigars were in the waste paper basket beneath the dressing table.

In the bathroom directly opposite the entrance to the master bedroom, he found a yellow towel with a small bloodstain lying on the side of the bath.

He took the following for forensic samples:

Contents of the glass on the bedside locker, thought to be milk

Cigar butt from the ashtray

Sellotape lift of pillows

Sellotape lift of hairs on the bed

Sample of stained carpet on left side of the bed

Blood stained yellow towel from the bathroom.

The "brass bedroom" at the end of the corridor – No. 2 on the Garda map – was known to be Niall's room, not No. 9. At the inquest, when Richard Flynn was questioned about Therese demanding he go down for another drink for all of them, he replied: "I said, 'I might as well go back to my own room.'" Whether this was merely a throwaway remark or carried greater meaning remains unclear.

DOWNSTAIRS

Det. Garda Sergeant Edwin Handcock from the Ballistics Section visited Kilcoursey House on 9 July. He recorded an oval-shaped table downstairs in the dining room that was supported by two legs, each with three feet radiating outwards, with a brass claw at the end. One of the feet was broken off the leg nearest the fireplace and a piece of folded cardboard had been placed beneath it for support. The broken piece of wood was lying on the mantelpiece.

In the TV room, he found a wooden framed coffee table with a glass top, which was broken into two main pieces and some smaller pieces. The two bigger pieces were resting against the wall, with slivers of glass lying on the carpet beneath the table. Small fragments were missing, and later found in a trailer outside in the rear yard. The table itself was cracked at the front of the frame.

Therese put the damage down to wedding guests in the dining room on Saturday, and over-excited nephews watching Wimbledon in the TV room on Sunday.

FORENSIC ASSESSMENT

According to the 2015 McGinn report, the forensic analysis of samples taken from the 1985 crime scene and individuals involved appeared to be incomplete.

The report found: "Notwithstanding that blood samples were taken from the scene and from members of the Flynn family, that various physical items were taken from the principal bedroom and from other rooms in the house; that numerous fingerprints were located in the bedroom; and that all these samples and findings were transmitted to the State Forensics Science Laboratory, presumably with a view to trying to ascertain who had been in the bedroom and elsewhere; there is a complete absence of any record of any scientific testing of the samples taken during the examination of the scene."

There were also no detailed notes analysing the blood spatters detected in Kilcoursey House or of any conclusions drawn from the patterns of blood found by Gardaí. "A full and careful analysis of the pattern of blood spatters might have assisted in confirming or dismissing some of the suggested theories," the McGinn report stated.

There was also no record or documentation to suggest that Gardaí carried out any tests on three drinking glasses or a partially consumed bottle of brandy found in the master bedroom or that fingerprints lifted from "different items" in the room were analysed or matched to anyone.

The extent of cross-matching blood samples taken from Richard and Therese Flynn was also unclear.

While some evidence of cross-matching blood samples was given at Mr Flynn's trial, the McGinn report found no documentation showing that blood samples were cross-checked with swabs taken from the scene or other exhibits.

At the time scientists relied on the rudimentary grouping of blood samples, as DNA profiling had yet to come into use.

As part of the TV documentary, the experts suggested, however, that this incomplete picture raised the possibility that some of the ungrouped blood stains may have originated from someone other than Richard or Therese, although they also accepted there was no definitive evidence of anyone else being present.

"I don't think Richard did it. He was heavily involved, but was he protecting Therese, or someone else?" suggested Dr Ciara Staunton.

There was blood on a yellow towel taken from the bathroom opposite the master bedroom. This was not Niall's, "but could have come from either Richard or Therese Flynn, containing a group present in both bloods and in approximately 17 percent of the population," according to the forensic report.

On this aspect, Angela commented: "Not all the blood present was fully grouped. Therefore, it was impossible to discount a further individual present and bleeding. Or not.

"It was somebody in this house, either a person admittedly present, or someone else. It didn't mean it wasn't from Richard or Therese.

"But as Richard said, 'I'm the culprit,' he either was responsible, or he was covering for someone."

Ciara added: "In theory, yes, there could have been someone else, particularly with Richard's willingness to admit to the crime early on, but there's no documented evidence."

On assessing the recreated bedroom scene and forensic evidence the experts came to a number of conclusions, which raised questions over the narrative that a row erupted over drink in the bedroom.

On this point, Angela remarked: "It's a ridiculous idea, this argument over someone getting a drink. Richard wasn't even in the prime position to get a drink. Niall was the one fully dressed and closest to the door at the time."

"Richard knocks out both his wife and Fr Niall. He goes to the bathroom, gets a glass of water, and throws it over both to revive them. Where did that happen? Fr Niall's wound was bleeding, it was a cream carpet, so where was the diluted bloodstain? Blood is extremely difficult to remove completely and there is no evidence of diluted blood anywhere on the cream bedroom carpet," she added.

"The leaf in Fr Niall's collar – where did that come from? There was foliage in the bathroom – plants – but there was no matching leaf, signs of a struggle or blood distribution consistent with an altercation, unless it was thoroughly cleaned. What I would have done is trawled the property until I found a match for that leaf, and that would potentially be another crime scene," she explained.

Angela added: "It would have been natural to ring an ambulance, but they didn't. At the inquest and trial, it was all about a heart attack and drink. Once there was an admission of guilt, the scenes were not considered to objectively prove or disprove Richard's version of events."

THE CRIME SCENE THAT GOT AWAY

Therese made two statements, on July 9 to Gardaí and July 14 through her solicitor. She also gave evidence at the inquest, but not the trial. In her first statement, she said she remembered Niall lying on the floor. "I tried for his pulse but I could not get any, I then tried to give him the kiss of life."

In her statement issued through her solicitor, she said: "My next memory is of waking up or regaining consciousness on the floor of the bedroom. Fr Molloy was lying on the floor, near the door. I was dazed and thought he must have passed out. I tried to lift him up and said he had better get to bed. He gave no sign of life. I tried to revive him. I listened for his heartbeat, but heard none, but I heard an awful gurgling sound."

At the inquest, she said she was close to the bed when she regained consciousness, and Niall was lying close to the door. She thought he was passed out and lifted him by the shoulder in an attempt to get him to bed.

In each of her statements and evidence, she said she was alone in the room when she regained consciousness, yet Richard claimed she came to when he splashed water on her.

On the night Niall died, Therese was removed from the crime scene before the Gardaí arrived. It was the following Tuesday, 9 July before they were able to visit her in Tullamore Hospital, so she was never examined forensically, apart from her clothing.

Dr Peter Greally admitted Therese between 3.15am and 3.30am. In Therese's medical report, there was a note of twice the normal alcohol limit in her blood, but no trace of a sedative being present. It is understood she was only given a sedative – Valium – after she was admitted to hospital.

During the post-mortem, the State Pathologist took, amongst other things, a blood sample and nail scrapings from both of Niall's hands. No such samples were ever taken from Richard and Therese.

Based on the available evidence, the experts did not rule out the possibility that Therese could have played a role in Niall's demise.

Was it possible that Therese took Niall by surprise with the first blow which would account for his lack of offensive or defensive injuries?

There was potentially a lot at stake, so did Therese feel threatened by the potential loss of face and reputation if word got out about the family's financial woes?

Richard's admission to being the 'culprit' may have also been a factor, Angela added: "Everybody is sort of 'It's terrible, it's horrendous but we've got our man; we don't really need to prove or disprove his version of events.'"

But the fact that Therese was not forensically examined represented a significant gap in the evidence.

"Nobody took nail clippings from Therese. Nobody looked at her nails to see if they were broken; to see if she had somebody else's skin cells under her nails if she had been fighting. We know she bled because her blood was present on Richard, but we don't know what her injury was.

"Richard's pyjama top is torn under the arm. The buttons had been pulled off; he's been grabbed. Think about if you've got a pyjama top on and the button gets pulled off and it's ripped; that's happened in an altercation. But it wasn't Fr Molloy because he's got no defence or offence injuries. Who else do we know is in this room? Therese, the fairer sex, she was a crime scene; she was the crime scene that got away."

Chapter 15
THE TRUTH WILL OUT?

It is July 2021, the 36th anniversary of Fr Niall Molloy's death. The numbers are down but, every year since 1985, family, friends and parishioners continue to congregate at the Church of the Assumption in Castlecoote to remember the man they knew and cherished. On this occasion, amidst the Covid-19 pandemic, the few familiar faces are hidden behind masks.

Despite the passage of time, Fr Molloy is ever-present. The reminders of his contribution and his passing are everywhere; the community hall he built for the parish of Fuerty, the bungalow his parishioners built for him, and his lone grave to one side of the church, where his faithful flock wanted it.

With every passing year, Fr Molloy's anniversary Mass triggers an all too familiar sense of frustration and unease. It also highlights the uncomfortable reality that justice has not been served.

Every year, family, friends and parishioners believe it might be the last anniversary they must endure without answers, but it never is.

Addressing the congregation, one of his nephews, Fr Billy Molloy recalled events of that summer Sunday 36 years previously:

"A gentle, kind and prayerful priest left his parishioners here to go to a wedding reception for people he had known, their daughter was after getting married. But he could never have imagined in his wildest dreams or his worst nightmare what the following hours would bring and the effect it would have on this parish community, the family, and the whole of Ireland. Beaten and kicked to death and left there on the ground as he struggled for life and for breath. But I know in my own heart, at the moment of death, he was not alone; Our Blessed Lady came and brought him home."

By 2022, there is a real sense of time running out, with his family and friends now in their seventies and eighties.

While many have reluctantly reached the point of acceptance that justice may never be served, the making of the TV documentary about the case offered fresh promise.

The hope was that someone would have the conscience to come forward with new information about what really transpired at Kilcoursey House on that July weekend in 1985. Nobody did.

A lot has happened with the Molloy case since but for Niall's family, very little has actually changed or progressed.

Bill Maher, who has fronted the Justice for Fr Niall Molloy campaign over the past decade, is now in his early seventies and fears he will not see closure in his lifetime.

He remains optimistic though that the next generation of Molloys will continue the quest for answers.

For those who knew Niall, it is unfinished business. For those who did not get the chance to know the gentle cleric, it is a matter of accountability, truth and justice.

As Niall's grandniece Maria Devane put it: "You have one set of people who are spending their whole lives covering up and you have another set of people grieving, forever looking for answers."

In September 2021, the two-part TV documentary *The Killing of Fr Niall Molloy* was broadcast on RTÉ One and repeated in early 2022.

Drawing on all available evidence and interviews with the Molloy family and parishioners of Castlecoote, among others who knew Niall, the fresh take on the cold case attracted widespread interest from the public and media alike.

The first episode secured the second-highest viewing numbers, after the *Late Late Show*, when aired on 6 September – something that few documentaries have achieved in recent years. It showed the public interest in the case, from those who remembered it, and those who were learning about it for the first time.

People could not fathom what had happened in 1985 and since then – from Richard Flynn's incredible account of events to the truncated trial and bizarre claims that Therese was a sibling of Niall's.

The sense of disbelief did not stop there as fresh questions arose over the fact that nobody has been held accountable for Niall's death to this day or taken responsibility for the shortcomings of the criminal justice system.

By replicating and building a set of the bedroom and ensuite at Kilcoursey House, forensic and crime scene experts were able to test the evidence given by Richard in 1985. In the end, they concluded that events could not have happened as described by him.

The documentary also shed new light on financial dealings between Fr Molloy and the Flynns, who owed him a significant

THE KILLING OF FR NIALL MOLLOY

amount of money, as well as the changing fortunes facing the Flynn family businesses at the time – none of which was fully probed or pursued in the 1980s.

When the TV documentary aired, there was no reaction from the authorities or witnesses involved. At the other extreme, the documentary team were contacted by people who claimed to have information, but much of it was unsubstantiated, fantasy or rumours that had already been heard and discounted.

Where the documentary was limited in terms of time, in this book we have detailed as much as possible, the full facts of what is known about how Niall died 37 years ago.

Since 1985 a Garda investigation, trial and inquest, followed by a fresh Garda examination and independent review, have all failed to draw a line under the suspicious circumstances of Fr Molloy's death.

After more than three decades, there are two key unresolved aspects to the Molloy case: the killing of Niall – who did it, how and why; and the aftermath of his death – the investigation, the trial, and new medical evidence that cast fresh doubt over the account put forward by Richard and Therese Flynn.

Available evidence suggests that Richard was involved in Niall's death and Therese was the only other person in the room.

There is also clear evidence that Richard owed Niall a significant sum of money and that, shortly before his death, the cleric sought legal advice about getting it back.

The evidence further suggests that Niall was killed on the night of 7 July into the morning of 8 July and that he took hours to die.

The sequence of events, actions of certain witnesses, and statements supplied to Gardaí have not been fully tested, either during the original investigation, the curtailed trial, or during the more recent Garda review. Of the 10-15 witnesses present in Kilcoursey House on the night Fr Molloy died, five have since passed away – May Quinn, Dr Daniel O'Sullivan, Fr James Deignan, and Therese and Richard Flynn – but the remaining witnesses could, under a Commission of Investigation, be questioned under oath, some for the first time.

Despite rumours of a cover-up being denied and dismissed, there are several glaring gaps and omissions in the hours, days, weeks, months and years that followed Fr Molloy's death.

For example, the original Garda investigation failed to obtain a copy of the wedding guest list for 6 July 1985 and failed to question all parties who attended and stayed late at the post-wedding lunch on Sunday, 7 July.

There are questions over why phone records for Kilcoursey House on the night were not checked or verified to establish who was called and when.

There are questions over the forensic analysis and the handling of Fr Molloy's watch – another potentially vital piece of evidence – which was returned to the family within days of his death.

Added to this is the "extraordinary" intervention of Judge Frank Roe at Richard Flynn's trial, which prevented any line of questioning about the failed land deal and monies owed and ultimately allowed the businessman to walk free on all charges.

Of even greater concern is the loss by Gardaí of records and potentially vital exhibits over the years, in a crime that remains unsolved. There is no record of how they were managed or how or when they disappeared.

There is clear evidence that Niall's family were let down by the criminal justice system – by gaps in the original investigation, a failure to include key witness statements in the Book of Evidence, and by Judge Roe in his ruling at trial.

Under the 2004 Commission of Investigation Act, a clear legal mechanism is available that could compel 'reluctant' witnesses to attend and provide evidence to a public inquiry under oath.

This has the potential to open up new avenues of investigation by calling witnesses who were present on the night of Fr Molloy's death and other persons of interest, as well as speaking to members of An Garda Síochána involved in the original investigation.

Here we detail the key questions and issues requiring further clarity:

THE FRIENDSHIP AND PARTNERSHIP: There are still some questions about the extent of the personal and business relationship between Fr Molloy and Richard and Therese Flynn. Even though the mention of the case elicits comments about an affair between Niall and Therese, there is no evidence or informed opinion to support such a theory. The business partnership between them was a lucrative one and they were well respected within the show jumping and bloodstock circuit. It is unlikely that they were caught in a "compromising position" given that the Flynns and Fr Molloy enjoyed a friendship of 28 years. At the same time, it was unusual for a friend to be so embedded in the family unit and household to the extent that Niall was, which may have been a source of discomfort for some.

THE JOINT ASSETS: Over the course of Niall and Therese's business partnership trading in horses, livestock and land, tens of thousands of pounds passed through their joint bank account. While the SCRT review verified elements of the business relationship it was not possible to establish a complete picture of their shared assets – although that opportunity was available in the 1980s when records were accessible and the Molloy family pressed for the case to be reopened on foot of fresh medical evidence. In the absence of documentation, lost, missing or unavailable, the full extent of Niall's assets – and their disposal – remains a mystery.

THE URGENT LAND DEAL: As part of the TV documentary, we discovered new information suggesting a sense of urgency around plans by Niall and Therese to purchase 38 acres of Kilcoursey land from Richard. The deal in 1984 was drawn up within 24 hours of another property transaction falling through. The trio were in the process of buying a house near Letterfrack in Connemara but a planning issue arose that resulted in a last-minute change of plan. The intended Letterfrack purchase, while unclear, made no sense as an investment as none of the parties had a link to the locality, even though both Richard and Therese were from Galway. It was also a very small land holding that would not have offered suitable terrain to breed horses. It is not clear if this information was available to Gardaí in 1985 but if it had it might also have changed the direction of the investigation.

THE FLYNN FINANCES: Outwardly, Richard and Therese Flynn were considered wealthy by 1980s standards. They ran a chain of motor accessory shops and a coffee shop in Athlone while Therese also pursued her interest in horses with Niall. As revealed in the documentary, however, there is some evidence to suggest that the

Flynn finances were on the wane from 1983 onwards. Annual returns for one of Richard's motor accessory businesses show that company debts grew from IR£23,110 in 1983 to IR£115,311 by 1986, while the Revenue Commissioners and Barclays Bank registered significant debts against the businessman by 1987. The rapidly rising debts lend some weight to the possibility that the Molloy-Flynn business partnership may have been in trouble at the time of Niall's death and that money may have been a factor. The financial dimension of this case, however, was not thoroughly investigated at a time when more documentation would have been available.

THE MISSING WILL: Despite the fact that Fr Molloy is believed to have made a will on at least two occasions – at the time of his Ordination in 1957 and before travelling to Cyprus in 1972 as Army Chaplain – no will has been found to date. The Diocese of Elphin, where the priest served, could not trace any record of Niall's will despite some evidence suggesting that he deposited it with a clerical colleague. The missing will has added to the mystery surrounding Fr Molloy's death. There are several reasons why the Church may not have wanted details of the will to be made public. Even though Niall was not obliged to take a vow of poverty, a curate with considerable wealth in 1985 would have attracted unwelcome attention for the Church. There was also the risk of embarrassment for the Church, if pressed to explain a wealthy priest leaving his assets to a woman, as was claimed.

THE MYSTERIOUS BURGLARY: Another event, not included in the original Garda investigation, was a mysterious break-in at the parochial house in Castlecoote in the months before Fr Molloy's death. It was never formally reported to Gardaí but Kierán Connell, the local Sergeant at the time, recalls approaching Niall about the burglary. The curate said he would check to see if anything was missing but seemed unconcerned and never followed up with a report. It was only after Fr Molloy's death, when business papers, bank statements, horse passports and other documents could not be found that Kierán and others recalled the strange incident. It was assumed the missing records were taken during the break-in.

THE MISSING HOURS: There were gaps in witness statements given to Gardaí that were never tested or challenged at Richard's trial, due to it being abruptly cut short by the presiding judge.

In statements from the Flynn family and the live-in groom, there is a discrepancy of 45 minutes.

Therese was seen making tea in the kitchen at Kilcoursey at 9pm and 9.20pm; along the road at 9.10pm and 9.40pm; and in Goodbodys at 9.10pm and 9.20pm. She cannot have been in all of those locations at all of those times.

Similarly, there was a discrepancy in the time Fr Deignan and the pub revellers returned to Kilcoursey from Tober House, where David and his wife, Ann, had entertained them after White's pub closed. According to statements, they arrived at any time between 1am and 1.45am.

Overall, there is an undisputed period of around two hours, where several people, including the parish priest and a local doctor, were in Kilcoursey House but had not alerted Gardaí to Fr Molloy's death or called an ambulance or emergency services.

THE SIBLING CONNECTION: During the documentary, two documents were uncovered that recorded Therese as Niall's sister, adding another layer of intrigue to the Molloy case. The first document was a life insurance policy in Niall's name that came to light in 1988, when Therese allegedly tried to cash it in. Another document relating to the proposed Connemara property deal in 1984 also named the businesswoman as Niall's sister.

THE MEDICAL EVIDENCE: There were gaps in the medical evidence. An analysis of brain tissue samples by Dr Michael Farrell was not included in evidence at Richard's trial. Decades later, the McGinn report said this represented a "major omission" by Gardaí and could have changed the complexion of the case. While the Molloy family were unaware of this omission at the time, they sought fresh medical evidence in 1988 which they brought to Gardaí. An independent assessment of Niall's brain tissue samples suggested he may have survived for hours after sustaining head injuries. With this new medical evidence, the family pushed for the case to be reopened to no avail. A number of independent pathologists subsequently analysed tissue samples supporting the theory that Niall was left to die for hours. If a new investigation had been mounted at the time, it would have opened up a new line of questioning over the timeframe of events on the night, something that was never tested.

THE TIME OF DEATH: While Fr Molloy's post-mortem could not be definitive about the time of death, it estimated that he died between 11pm on Sunday night and 5am the following morning. Witness statements further suggest that Niall was dead at 1am when Maureen Parkes checked his pulse and covered his face with a towel. As stated above, repeated examinations of pathology slides confirmed that Niall was alive for several hours before he died, raising further doubts about the timeline of events. The possibility that Niall may have survived for at least two hours would suggest he was attacked before 11pm. His damaged watch – stopped at 10.40 – could also have represented a vital piece of evidence. It was, however, handed back to the Molloy family after the post-mortem and subsequently dismissed as evidence by the coroner at Niall's inquest.

THE INVESTIGATION SHORTCOMINGS: In 1985, Gardaí had limited powers of arrest and detention, which no doubt had an impact on their ability to detain and question suspects as part of any criminal investigation. It is of concern though that Gardaí failed to carry out a number of rudimentary tasks, such as house-to-house enquiries, in their investigation of Niall's death. These gaps – identified as shortcomings in the 2015 McGinn report – could have been critical to the investigation, in particular the "significant omission" of including a statement from Fr Molloy's solicitor about the collapsed land deal in the Book of Evidence. The issue of money was cited as a potential motive, a key factor that could have changed the course of the trial. There is no evidence that Gardaí spoke to or took statements from other potential witnesses, including the two best men who were staying at Tober House and the wedding guests, a couple, who were friends with the Flynn siblings, and were supposed to stay at Kilcoursey House on the night.

THE INCOMPLETE FORENSICS: There is also an incomplete forensic picture despite a multitude of samples being taken from the crime scene and from the parties involved. The McGinn report found "a complete absence of any record of any scientific testing" of samples. Equally of concern was a lack of any detailed notes analysing the blood spatters detected in Kilcoursey House or of any conclusions drawn from the patterns of blood found by Gardaí. There are no records either to say whether other exhibits or fingerprint samples from the crime scene were tested or analysed. Questions also remain over why certain forensic evidence was not pursued or interrogated in greater detail. For example, the leaf that was found in Niall's shirt collar that night did not appear to be considered as part of the investigation. There are questions, too, over the button from Richard's pyjamas, found on the floor of the master bedroom – it had been ripped from his pyjama top but by whom and how?

THE MISSING EVIDENCE: Despite the considerable volume of samples and exhibits, not one piece of evidence remains today, nor is there any record of it. According to Chief Superintendent Christopher Mangan, several Garda stations were searched, to no avail. There is no report of what happened to this evidential material and questions remain over the Garda management and handling of evidence that could prove vital in an unsolved death. As the law stands today, the SCRT, or GSOC, do not have the power to question retired members of the force.

THE TRIAL AND INQUEST: Critical questions also remain over Judge Frank Roe's intervention in the 1986 trial of Richard, who was charged with manslaughter and assault causing harm to Niall. In an extraordinary intervention, Judge Roe accepted defence submissions that Fr Molloy could have died from a heart attack and not the serious head injuries he had sustained. His decision curtailed the trial and prevented other witnesses being called or other issues, such as the failed land deal and monies owing to Niall, being examined or tested. Decades later, Judge Roe was found to have misapplied the law. Within weeks of the trial, a sworn inquest into Fr Molloy's death turned the trial outcome on its head and found that he had in fact died of head injuries.

THE BROKEN FURNITURE: There are questions, too, over the broken furniture discovered downstairs in Kilcoursey House and whether it was thoroughly investigated at the time. Gardaí were aware of the broken dining table and coffee table when the case went to trial and did examine the furniture as part of their investigation. The issue, however, took on greater significance at the subsequent inquest when Dr O'Sullivan gave evidence of a row also taking place downstairs. The family doctor also raised the possibility that Fr Molloy fell against the fireplace. Therese, however, told the inquest that the dining room table had been broken by a guest on the day of the wedding and the coffee table had been broken by nephews when watching tennis that Sunday. At no point were these claims tested.

THE OTHER QUESTIONS: While Richard confessed to being the "culprit" and involved in Niall's death, that admission was never queried, fully tested or challenged. It is also curious that some witnesses described him as calm or composed while others said he was visibly distressed on the night. There is also a question over Therese's hazy account of events, in particular whether she had taken a sleeping pill and a nightcap before retiring to bed. When Dr O'Sullivan arrived on the scene, Therese was in a hysterical state and he testified to treating her, although he never said what that entailed. It is understood that no sedative was detected when Therese was admitted to hospital but that she was subsequently given one.

THE ALTERNATIVE THEORIES: From the time Fr Molloy's death became news, the local community of Clara had their own theory about what might have happened. One witness allegedly confided in a friend that the events of the night Niall died were not as Richard stated but they subsequently denied making such claims. Another theory was that the post-wedding lunch on Sunday was still in full swing long after 6pm, with many guests in Kilcoursey House after 9pm. Another witness claims to have seen Niall on his horse and cart between 9pm and 9.30pm that Sunday, adding to doubts over events that night. It was also suggested that when Niall returned from his jaunt around the village of Clara, he spent some time in the stables, looking after his horses. The theory is that he was allegedly struck to the head and knocked unconscious while in the stables and that he was then carried through the house and brought upstairs to the master bedroom. Little evidence has been offered to substantiate this theory, although the discovery of a leaf in Fr Molloy's shirt collar does raise some questions. Gardai also investigated the potential existence of a recording of a phone conversation between a potential witness, who allegedly confided, years later, in a friend about events on the night. No recording has come to light to date.

THE QUESTION OF A COVER-UP: The idea that the Church, State and Judiciary colluded to cover up the truth about the death of

Fr Molloy has been rumoured and dismissed in equal measure. Unsurprisingly, there is no evidence to support the allegation.

At a time when the nation was still enraptured by Catholicism, the Church feared a scandal. After administering the Last Rites to Fr Molloy that night the local parish priest, Fr Deignan, returned to the parochial house and allegedly called his bishop for advice.

The issue was touched on by local parishioner and journalist James Gibbons in the documentary.

"I remember some years later because I was very friendly with Fr Deignan. I asked about the whole Flynn case, that was how it was sort of referred to in the town, and he said that he telephoned Mullingar and when Fr Deignan referred to Mullingar, he meant the Bishop," Mr Gibbons recalled.

It is also worth bearing in mind that Fr Deignan had his own legal representative at the inquest and that under questioning he declined to divulge any aspects of his conversation with Richard Flynn on the night.

"He knew it was going to be a huge scandal for the Church and we know now that the church tries to avoid scandal. He took advice and then of course he took legal advice and was legalled up to the hilt when he was in the witness box," he added.

There is also evidence that Fr Deignan subsequently asked Sgt Forde to keep Niall's death quiet.

Apart from the current Bishop of Elphin, Rev. Kevin Doran, there was little by way of support from the Church for the Molloy family and their quest for answers, despite Niall being one of their own.

There have also been other allegations of interference down through the years. Such as claims that Judge Roe wrote to the DPP about a conflict of interest and that he knew both Fr Molloy and the Flynns. These claims have not been backed up by hard evidence nor have they been wholly disproved. A Commission of Investigation, however, has the potential to shed new light on certain aspects of how the Molloy case was handled by Gardaí and Judge Roe.

###

THE CAMPAIGN FOR JUSTICE

A common thread running through this tragic case, is the fact that the Molloy family repeatedly met with resistance in their quest for justice over the past 37 years.

They pushed for the case to be reopened in 1988 when they obtained new medical evidence suggesting that Niall may have survived for several hours before dying that night. That was a significant revelation and raised serious questions over the account of events given by several witnesses. Nothing came of it, however, at a critical time when business records and dealings could have been thoroughly examined.

The Molloy family also hit another roadblock when they made repeated attempts to obtain a copy of the transcript of Richard Flynn's trial in 1986, which was abruptly cut short by Judge Roe. They were repeatedly advised that, because there was no appeal, the hearing was not transcribed and a transcript did not exist.

In 2019, however, family members were tipped off by a journalist, who had sight of the trial transcript. Yet again, the family sought a copy but were advised it did not exist. It was only when the family informed the newly appointed President of the Circuit Court, Judge Patricia Ryan, of its existence that they managed to obtain a copy. Judge Ryan, coincidentally whose in-laws were Brian and

Anne Lenihan, tracked it down and supplied the transcript with an apology. Its typeface and format suggested that the transcript was transcribed in the late 1980s and was there all along.

Requests by the family for documents about the case under the Freedom of Information (FOI) Act also failed to bear much fruit. A 2014 FOI request to the Department of Justice for any documents relating to the case was partially granted but any released documents did not predate 2010. The family appealed the FOI decision and sought clarification on documents dating back to the 1980s while also taking a case to the Information Commissioner.

In 2015, the Department confirmed that following a manual trawl of its archives, records and documents from the 1980s were located. "I must apologise that these documents were not considered in relation to your original FOI request. It appears that details of the particular file were omitted in error when archived material was recorded in the Department's electronic file database," a Departmental official wrote in a letter to the family.

Even after the toing and froing, only some documents were released to the Molloy family but nothing of consequence, with their efforts merely returning much of the correspondence submitted by family members or local TDs to various Justice Ministers over the years.

While some documents, such as those relating to the Attorney General or DPP, could not be released under the FOI Act, the Department refused to release other records on the grounds of legal privilege or that it would not be in the public interest. Looking back on the SCRT review, Bill Maher, one of the Molloy relatives at the helm of the family's campaign for justice, described the cold case review as in-depth with a strong recommendation for further inquiry.

"The cold case review was quite thorough and considered Fr Niall's death to be murder. In the end, it recommended a Commission of Investigation as the only way to compel witnesses to cooperate and the only way of getting to the truth," Mr Maher said.

The subsequent review of the SCRT probe by Senior Counsel Dominic McGinn, however, did little to advance the Molloy family's quest for justice.

When the McGinn review was announced in December 2013, the Molloy family gave it a cautious welcome. They were not consulted on the terms of reference but any concerns fell on deaf ears and the review was confined to the SCRT findings.

The terms of reference also came with the caveat that, if recommended, any further inquiry would require a "reasonable prospect of establishing the truth". In the end, Mr McGinn concluded that this was "unlikely" and ruled out any further inquiry.

Yet again, it was one step forward, two steps back for the Molloy family. The case had been re-investigated by Gardaí and a senior legal expert had reviewed the findings of the fresh Garda probe. Both exercises, however, were hindered by either investigative limitations or a narrow scope for inquiry.

Commenting on the McGinn report, Mr Maher said: "It was useful in some respects but there are several aspects of the report which we do not regard as an accurate reflection of the evidence that is available. It remains unclear if Mr McGinn had access to all available documents or merely a summary of the SCRT findings."

In the wake of the McGinn report, the Molloy family again pushed for a full Commission of Investigation, which they felt could address many of the limitations and snags identified and potentially remedy the injustices and failings that were uncovered.

Despite the clear shortcomings and deficiencies in the original Garda investigation, the Fine Gael-led Government of the day dismissed the fresh calls for a public inquiry, relying on the conclusion of the McGinn report.

In the end, the Molloy family was compelled to make a complaint to the Garda Siochána Ombudsman Commission (GSOC), which was damning in its 2018 findings, in particular over the loss of potentially vital exhibits and evidence.

Yet again the Molloy case was generating headlines but making very little progress. Speaking to *Morning Ireland* on RTÉ Radio 1 in 2018, Henry McCourt said the family were deeply disappointed by the GSOC report findings.

"Documents and exhibits which could well have been extremely important as a result of advances in DNA science... have disappeared. All of the exhibits have disappeared and a considerable amount of documents have disappeared," Mr McCourt said, adding that there was no log or record of where the documents or exhibits went.

In response the then Minister for Justice, Charlie Flanagan, issued a statement committing to bring forward proposals to give GSOC the power to interview retired Gardaí. Four years on, these powers have not yet materialised.

Today, in 2022, the Molloy case remains unsolved and officially open, and, despite the many setbacks and roadblocks, Niall's family are refusing to give up. They continue to hold out hope of getting closer to the truth, perhaps against all odds.

Since the SCRT and McGinn reviews, the government has sent clear signals that it has no intention of granting a Commission of Investigation into the Molloy case.

In the wake of the recent TV documentary, Sinn Féin's Justice spokesperson Martin Kenny made renewed calls for a full investigation into the case in the Dáil in September 2021.

"If we remember, at the same time in the mid-1980s, how the family of Joanne Hayes in County Kerry was treated, we will note the stark contrast between a poor family and a wealthy family and how they were treated by the State. It is something that slaps us all in the face and should wake us up to what needs to happen here," the Leitrim-based TD said.

"There needs to be a full investigation into how this happened. The only way that can be done is through a Commission of Investigation that will compel people to tell the truth about what happened. It is a scandal that has gone on for too long," he added.

Junior Minister for Justice, Fianna Fáil TD James Browne, once again ruled out any further inquiry but did acknowledge the shortcomings in the original Garda investigation.

"The report by Mr McGinn outlines how some of the concerns expressed regarding this case were not supported by evidence. It details shortcomings in the original investigation, which were identified by the SCRT review," Minister Browne said.

He then repeated the government line taken in 2015 on foot of the McGinn report, which concluded that the precise events surrounding Fr Molloy's death could not be ascertained. The Minister also pointed out that the investigation into the death of Fr Molloy remains open and that anyone with any relevant information should contact Gardaí.

Deputy Kenny, however, continued to point out that several other families have been let down by the State: "The manner in which the case was hushed up is really what needs to be examined. Anyone with an ounce of common sense will realise that the only way this can be done, and the only way we can get to the truth here, is by compelling people to tell the truth and to speak clearly and openly at a Commission of Investigation. It is simply not good enough that the family has been let down. It is not the only one. There are many other families in similar circumstances around the country."

The authors of this book have lived with this story, and all of its twists and turns, for a few short years. For the Molloy family, the quest for answers is now approaching four decades and continues to take its toll.

"It's not just Niall; it's the knock-on effect it's had on the rest of the family over the years. I lost my parents within three years. I lost my uncle shortly after Niall. I lost my brother and the family would reckon that the case cost him his premature life because he got so obsessed by it and kept chasing, and ultimately, he died, he died young," Bill Maher told the documentary.

Even if the truth cannot be borne out, the many injustices in the case cannot simply be ignored or dismissed.

The McGinn report identified a series of critical shortcomings in the 1985 Garda investigation, such as the failure to include a statement from Fr Molloy's solicitor in the Book of Evidence or to seek and include the opinion of Dr Michael Farrell in evidence in relation to the time of death. These were potentially significant pieces of information that could have changed the course of the investigation and ultimately the criminal trial.

These shortcomings, among others, have merely been acknowledged by the State as deficiencies or errors and have been left hanging in the air.

No apology or remedy has been offered to the Molloy family for how the case was handled by Gardaí and the criminal justice system.

With limited powers, GSOC could not investigate the family's complaint about the substandard investigation and could not question retired members of the force.

Now, 37 years on, the family have to live with the fact that Gardaí lost evidence down through the decades – a fate that other families in similar circumstances may also face.

In March 2022, Henry McCourt wrote to the Justice Minister Helen McEntee again calling for an inquiry into how Fr Molloy's death was handled.

Appealing for a meeting with the Justice Minister, Mr McCourt wrote: "I see no reason why a Commission of Investigation over a short period of time could not be held in relation to this matter."

"The State now wishes to continue to take the stance that whilst the facts of the case are most unfortunate and regrettable, it would prefer to do nothing," he added.